Losing My Religion

The Story of My Life

By Amy Mercer

Dedicated to…

My husband, Lee – who is, without a doubt, my best friend and greatest supporter.

Our sons, Luke and Joseph – who are the most wonderful gifts I could have ever asked for.

My pastors and leaders, both current and former – who have poured a wealth of love and grace into my life.

My family and friends – who have loved me unconditionally.

Table of Contents

Prologue

Prologue

When I was in college, some friends and I would meet on Tuesday evenings at a local watering hole called High on Rose, named for the fact that the bar was situated on the corner of High Street and Rose Street in the university district of Lexington, Kentucky. Almost weekly we gathered around one of the rustic wooden tables and listened to a live acoustic performance while snacking on chips, salsa, and beer.

It was there that I first heard a rendition of the classic John Prine folk song "Paradise," with the famous line "Daddy, won't you take me back to Muhlenberg County." My friends and I would sing the song over and over, week after week, and although it may seem cliché, the nostalgic lyrics stirred a longing in my soul.

Little did I know that one of the stops on my roller coaster journey would in fact be an old coal mining town situated in none other than Muhlenberg County, Kentucky, the very area that was the subject of this folksy tune. When I arrived alone in that isolated place a number of years later at the age of 27, I found that it was a far cry from the semi-metropolitan lifestyle I had once enjoyed. But this seemingly insignificant place in the middle of the rolling hills of Western Kentucky would prove to be a place of great transition in my life. Not only would I meet my husband there, but more importantly, I would encounter my Creator.

The first two lines of the song's chorus are as follows:

Daddy won't you take me back to Muhlenberg County
Down by the Green River where Paradise lay?

In the song, Paradise refers to the small town that was the center of excavation by the prosperous Peabody Coal Company in the middle of the twentieth century. But I have to ask myself if I was, in reality, making a prophetic cry to my real Father in heaven as I raised my voice to sing the lyrics of this classic song. Is it possible that I was crying to Him to take me to a place where I would find my own paradise, which was nothing less than the peace and rest I had been seeking all of my life—the peace and rest that I eventually found in a man named Jesus?

Before I opened my heart to Christ, I allowed myself to be temporarily satisfied by counterfeit forms of freedom. I believed that a life without boundaries would satisfy my desire for a fulfilling existence. Many periods of severe darkness proved my theory was incorrect.

I had a taste of true freedom in the cleansing I received from my Creator. When I knew beyond a shadow of a doubt that I was forgiven of all my sin and shame and that my life was reconciled to God, my journey toward freedom began. And that is what this book is all about – a journey.

It is about what happens when we walk away from the *good* kind of religion (acknowledgement of the divine or sacred), and it is also about the liberation found in walking away from the *bad* kind of religion (the ritualistic act of trying to win God's approval in our own strength).

It is about a journey toward everything the human heart longs for – peace, purpose, and freedom. Contained within my account are all the trappings of the typical rescue story…a girl carried away by addiction, depression, and aggression. And yet, my story is not typical at all. If it were, I would not have bothered to write it.

Part I

The Journey Begins

Chapter 1

Losing My Sanity

My mind it was mangled, I ran into the night.

BOB DYLAN

But one night I had a dream that frightened me; I saw visions that terrified me as I lay in my bed.

DANIEL 4:5 NLT

Ours is a culture in which the inappropriate use of words and phrases is very common. We say things we don't really mean. We say we love ice cream, and only a moment later say we love our husband or our wife, as though ice cream and the ones we love come anywhere close in value and importance. Another example of our misappropriation of words is the phrase "losing our minds." We ask, "Have you lost your mind?" when someone makes a decision we think is foolish. Or we may walk into a room and not remember why we're there or what we're looking for. Verdict: "I must be losing my mind."

But in 1996, around the month of August, I literally lost my mind. My mental processes were no longer my own. I had truly lost my own mind. And while it would be impossible to give a quick and

1

accurate psychological assessment of what occurred, I can explain the experience in a simple way. Imagine that your inner being, the very person you are, was somehow placed inside the mind of someone else. Imagine you have only a vague memory of the way that you used to think, while you're being dominated with new thoughts that are foreign, tortured, and bizarre. Imagine your mental processes becoming so twisted that the inevitable outcome is a mind that has moved beyond the hope of a return to sanity. Imagine becoming mentally trapped and tormented, with no conceivable way of escape.

That is the best way to describe what happened to me in August of 1996 and in the months following. I never expected to come to a place where I would have exchanged my life for nearly anyone else's on the planet. I never would have imagined that this low level of despair, loneliness, and utter helplessness could be reached. But I found myself in a state of mind that at one time would have been beyond my wildest imagination. It was a place where few have gone, and where none have gone by conscious choice.

To the best of my ability, I have attempted to explain the detours of life that led me down this dark and destructive path. I have done my best to capture as many necessary details as possible. However, certain periods of my journey are vague. Memories of certain times and events are not completely clear. You will soon understand why. But I have attempted to do justice in sharing the details of my seemingly narrow escape. The fact that I am "in my right mind," telling you the details of my liberation, is truly a miracle, as you will soon see.

Birth and Early Childhood

On a snowy morning in February, my mother gave birth to a healthy seven-pound girl. I barely missed being born in the 60s. The year was 1970. I was my parents' second child. My sister Jill had been born nearly five years prior, and my sister Dana would be born just 19 months later. Being the middle child in a family of three girls was a running joke of mine for many years. I called it the "Jan Brady Syndrome." If you know much about the 1970's television show *The Brady Bunch*, you will understand the humor. Jan Brady was the middle child, also born between her two sisters. Her character often faced troubles because of her place in the family. In fiction, the middle child is often portrayed as the one who struggles most with emotional growth and social interaction. This, of course, is a stereotype; however, it was true in my case. It always seemed as though I was the one in the family who struggled both socially and emotionally.

My place of origin happened to be a mid-sized western Kentucky town, located directly across the Ohio River from southern Indiana. Surrounded by corn, soybeans, and tobacco crops, the town prided itself on local sports, politics, and world-famous barbeque. Although our city was loved by many of its inhabitants, my sentiments were different. Somewhere in my mind, my birthplace seemed largely disconnected from the world at large. It often felt as though the rest of humanity was experiencing an abundance of what the world had to offer, while our community was lingering in passivity and isolation. Even as a child, I felt there had to be more to life than what I was encountering.

This perception may have been partially due to the geographic location of the town, which was disconnected from any interstates or major highways. Or maybe I watched too many movies and too much television and had an unrealistic expectation about what life was supposed to be. Some say that people who watch so much television do so because they want to connect with humanity and cannot seem to do so in their current existence. Then again, maybe my feeling of disconnectedness had little to do with my geographic location or with the culture I was in. Maybe it was something else.

Hometown Life

My father was a hard worker and a good supporter. He and I were very close, because I was the tomboy of the family. Together, we spent time playing ball and going on errands.

My father was involved in a number of business ventures in addition to his regular occupation in the steel industry. He was co-owner of several liquor stores and a number of racing horses. I would often tag along with Dad when he went to the liquor stores to take care of the bookkeeping.

On some Saturdays, we went to the racetrack where I attempted to master the skill of reading a racing form. After my very amateur study of the statistical information, I would run to the ticket window to place a bet. In those days, a young child could walk right up to a betting booth and put money on a horse. After placing my two-dollar bet, I marched to the grandstand and prepared for a minute and a half of excitement. I cheered for my selected horse as loudly as all of the adult gamblers who surrounded me.

The smell of booze, cigars, and burning pipes was a regular part of the racetrack scene, and it was the one part that I didn't like as a child. I am grateful that my father was always a sober man, but I was still uneasy and uncomfortable around adults who didn't seem able to control their thirst for alcohol.

While my father was a good provider and a lot of fun to be with, my mother was an excellent caregiver. She was always gentle and loving and did her best to make her three girls happy. Holidays and birthdays were always special because of Mom's loving touch. She wanted everything to be perfect. Although she herself was raised in a less-than-perfect home, she has always had a special amount of grace and class about her. And like my father, she herself did not drink alcohol. In fact, her term for alcohol was "poison." During her childhood, she had seen enough of its negative effects. Unfortunately, I did not share their wisdom about the potential dangers of chronic drinking, but I am grateful for parents who were sober all of my life.

I was a happy child in some sense of the word. I savored childhood play and had a great love for people. I spoke my first sentence at nine months of age. My parents said that it was almost scary how quickly I learned to talk. But I also experienced a lot of mental battles. As early as five or six years of age, it was difficult for me to fall asleep at night, and I would toss and turn for hours. I can remember being anxious and uneasy on various occasions, my imagination wandering into the possibility of tragic situations. As a result, I lived with an irrational fear of disaster. Sometimes panic would set in during a severe thunderstorm or a tornado watch, even though I had never been harmed by either of these.

A certain recurring image haunted me night after night as I lay in my bed trying to go to sleep. I would first visualize myself lying on the bed. Then I would see an image of the bed melting and turning into a jelly-like substance. After that, my mind would form a mental picture of the bed being sucked into the earth with me on it. I seemed to have no power to stop these mental "videos." I tried to retrain my mind to see myself lying in a bed that remained solid and firm, but it never worked. It was frightening, and I felt powerless to stop it. This continued for a number of years—my nightly appointment with torment—and it was just the beginning of things to come.

Chapter 2

High School in the 80s

If someone puts you down
That's so high school
Believing they're too cool for you
That's so high school
And when you believe it too
That's also high school
                    SUPERCHICK

Do not remember the rebellious sins of my youth.
Remember me in the light of your unfailing love,
for you are merciful, O LORD.
                    PSALM 25:7 NLT

It was my freshman year of high school and one of my classmates invited me to her house for an unsupervised party with her older sister and lots of eleventh and twelfth graders from our school. We sat around the kitchen table as I played my first drinking game. During the game of "Quarters," I was the target all the older kids aimed for. It was probably funny for them to watch a thin, young freshman girl put away as much alcohol as the 200-pound high school boys sitting around the table. As a result of their targeting me, I was

7

obligated to chug down glass after glass of beer. It didn't take long to get used to the taste, and I immediately loved the effects. After that key event, I looked forward to any chance to drink again.

Freshman year presented a whirlwind of challenges. Even though I appeared to adapt well on the outside, on the inside I felt alone and overwhelmed by the social pressures. Plus, I had a deep feeling that there had to be more to life than gossip and small talk. I was like an alien accidentally placed on the wrong planet. I was full of insecurity and was looking for something to fill the void in my soul.

Until high school I attended a small Catholic parochial school for eight years, where I enjoyed the comfort of being in class with the same students year after year. There, I was a model student who strived to be a "good kid." But high school was a huge new world full of peer pressure, dating, and popularity contests.

Beer and liquor, in my thinking, were a great way to have fun, get rid of the feelings of inadequacy, and forget about my pain. Even at my first drinking party, I was putting away more booze than most of the others there. This would continue to be a trend for me; one or two drinks were just never enough.

Since our school was a private, Catholic high school, we had kids from the city and the country. On most weekends, there was a party somewhere, often in an open field with coolers full of beer. And every year, I spent Spring Break in Florida, usually unsupervised and on a drinking rampage with other teenagers.

There was an emptiness that lingered in my soul. Growing up in the Me Decade didn't create an atmosphere that encouraged the pursuit of spiritual things. The search for spiritual fulfillment was secondary to the pursuit of worldly pleasures and honors.

Year after year, I excelled academically. Learning had always come easy to me. I loved books and I was an enthusiastic student in nearly every subject; however, I could not always handle the self-imposed pressure to make good grades. Pressure and stress ruled me most of the time. Even my kindergarten teacher had said I was too much of a perfectionist.

I certainly wasn't lazy—at least not about most things. I was active in sports and activities and had the appearance of an all-American girl. I spent much of my summertime at basketball camps and practices. I put this same work ethic into drinking.

Fortunately, during my high school years I never got out of control with my partying—at least not to the point that I was unable to function in day-to-day activities. This kind of trouble would come later. But the path to destruction had begun, and my gentle stroll would eventually evolve into a mad dash to insanity.

Chapter 3

End of Innocence

No security of mind is so salutary as that of innocence; guilt, however confident, has inexorable fears.

NORMAN MACDONALD, *MAXIMS AND MORAL REFLECTIONS*

Don't let the excitement of youth cause you to forget your Creator.

ECCLESIASTES 12:1 NLT

The neon lights on the main strip of Daytona Beach's party atmosphere provided a much more lively experience than the party scene I was used to in Kentucky. It was Spring Break, and rumor had it that one drunk college student had already plummeted from a condominium balcony. On the strip, horns were honking, music was blaring, people were shouting, and my friend and I were being scolded by the police for jaywalking. Two prostitutes standing on the corner laughed at our inexperience on the streets. I was barely fifteen, and I was hundreds of miles away from home and any parental guidance.

A friend had invited me to go to Florida with her. Her older sister and brother-in-law drove us there and were our chaperones, but not much was off limits. I was already accustomed to underage drinking, but illegal drugs were not something I anticipated encountering on the trip. Our first night there, a couple of older girls from our hometown visited our rented condo, and out came the marijuana. Everyone was ready to partake, except for me. Smoking pot would eventually become familiar territory, but as a somewhat naive suburban teen, I was overwhelmed by the experience.

The older girls taunted and teased me, trying to get me to smoke their weed. Instead I got extremely drunk, blacked out, and later found myself outside of the condo near the open air stairwell, not quite sure how I had gotten there. I wanted to go home. I hated being surrounded by people who regarded my safety and security as insignificant. And the worst part was that I had to endure it for a whole week.

On the way back to Kentucky, our vehicle got a flat tire. I didn't think I could take any more delays. Even though God and I weren't exactly tight, I begged Him to help me get home soon.

I never told my parents what took place on the trip. I wasn't innocent. I had been guilty of underage drinking for some time, but I was grateful to be back in familiar territory, knowing I could make it home when I needed to.

I continued to drink when the opportunities came around, still maintaining the illusion of being in control. I was able to function

11

from day to day and accomplish what I needed to do for school and extra-curricular activities.

However, my depression increased, though usually hidden beneath a crowd-pleasing smile. During school lunch break, I often went into a restroom stall to cry my eyes out. There were many days when I was suicidal and didn't want to go on with life and the loneliness of my existence. Although I had friends to hang out with, I never felt comfortable confiding in anyone.

My situation became a demonstration that popularity and worldly success do not guarantee happiness. In my case, I enjoyed an ample share of both. I also had my fair share of boyfriends, but these relationships were never satisfying either.

I had difficulty dealing with the unspoken expectation that dating a popular guy in high school meant eventually having sex with him. Though I was not exempt from a certain compulsion to give into the hormonal urges of teenage boys, there was a part of me that wasn't willing to succumb to their demands. I just wasn't comfortable with the pressure to engage in sex at that age. And the irony is that my conviction to do the right thing is what nearly destroyed me. Let me explain.

I felt like I was in a no-win situation. If I did not have sex, I could not date the most popular guys (or so it seemed), which made me feel inadequate in my circle of friends. If I did give in and have sex, I risked pregnancy, sexually transmitted disease, and a loss of my soul. (By "loss of my soul," I mean an aspect of my personality—my mind and my emotions—would have been compromised by going against my conviction about what was right.) But either way, I would lose.

My pattern of dating went something like this: I went out with nice-looking guys until the pressure rose to go further than I was comfortable going. I would then break off the relationship, though I did not necessarily want to lose the companionship of that person. But there was something in me that refused to allow my body to be used by a high school boy whom I was not likely to date forever. Even though my moral standards were not very high when it came to a lot of things, there was something in me that refused to be a mere object used for someone else's gratification.

There was also something deeper and troubling going on with my sexuality and my understanding of whom I was. Since third grade, I had secretly struggled with same-sex attraction. It ruled much of my thought life. I will discuss this later, as it didn't become a way of life until my college years.

In many ways I was living a double life, which would be my way of coping for years to come. I had a tendency to do one thing while being watched by those in authority, and to do another thing when I was with my friends who liked to party. But I would eventually find that living a double life places a huge demand on your soul.

Chapter 4

Leaving for College

No man should escape our universities without knowing how little he knows.

J. ROBERT OPPENHEIMER

We, of course, have plenty of wisdom to pass on to you once you get your feet on firm spiritual ground, but it's not popular wisdom, the fashionable wisdom of high-priced experts that will be out-of-date in a year or so. God's wisdom is something mysterious that goes deep into the interior of his purposes.

1 CORINTHIANS 2:6-8 MSG

A huge smile emerged on my face as I threw a tasseled graduation cap into the air as high as my arm muscles would allow. My family later told me they had never seen me look happier than during that classic moment at my senior commencement ceremony, when all of the graduates formed a large circle and uniformly tossed their caps in the air, giving a happy farewell to the high school years.

For me it meant a chance to leave the confines of the town I'd lived in for eighteen years. A chance to encounter a little more of the world. A chance to experience a diversity of culture and people. I wanted to know what it was like to live in a larger city and meet people from all walks of life. I wanted experiences like those I read about, heard about, and saw in movies.

I graduated near the top of my class and had several scholarship offers. I accepted a full-tuition scholarship to the University of Kentucky and entered my freshman year of college the next fall, majoring in biotechnology with the intention of going to medical school after graduation. During the first few semesters at UK, I made the dean's list and was a top student in all the science disciplines. During my freshman year, I ranked at the top of my class in chemistry and advanced biology. I even had the opportunity to study under the university's medical school professors, along with other pre-med students. During my sophomore year, I was ranked second out of about 260 physics students. On paper, my life looked pretty good.

I had a very competitive nature. My participation in college courses was no exception. I prided myself on the fact that I never attended chemistry lecture, but simply taught myself from the textbook, making nearly perfect scores on the tests. I spent a lot of time comparing scores with fellow pre-med students who were as competitive as I. There was a group of us who always tried to outdo one another in chemistry, biology, and calculus. These were all of my "geek" friends.

I had also joined a sorority, in which I made a lot of friends. And there were plenty of people to party with. In fact, before classes started at the beginning of my freshman year, the older girls in the sorority took all of the new "pledges," as we were called, to a big keg party with lots of boys and even more beer. At eighteen, I was like a freight train with no tracks to keep me on course.

Sorority life didn't really suit my nonconformist nature, yet I felt inclined to join. I had mainly taken an interest in joining a Greek organization due to pressure from others who said that being in a sorority would make it easier to make friends in a 25,000-plus university population. And they were right.

All of those desiring to pledge a sorority arrived a week early for college in order to go through "rush," the process through which sororities choose their members. Before classes started, we were under pressure to make a good impression in order to be invited back to the top sororities on campus. I went through the week with a smile on my face. It wasn't a smile of warm sincerity, contentment, happiness, or joy. Instead, it was an effort to make a good impression on all of those around me. It was my way of communicating that I had my act together. In other words, I allowed my face to provide a lot of false information. My Academy Award-winning performance paid off: I was continually invited back to the sorority houses of my choice.

Once I joined a sorority, I felt forced to keep up the good impression I made during rush. It wasn't enough to look good for a week. I had to keep up appearances with this group of young women on a regular basis. As a result, I always had an underlying fear that people would reject me if they knew who I really was.

There were some wonderful young women in my sorority and I made some very good friends, many I admire to this day. However, I had still not found that longed for freedom to be myself. Once again, I felt out of place much of the time. Once again, drinking became my liquid crutch to deal with all of the pressure.

University life made drinking extremely easy and accessible. No longer were there curfews or accountability. We were free to come and go from our dorms as we pleased. Just yards from my freshman dorm sat Fraternity Row, with its many parties night after night, week after week. Beer and liquor were not only easy for an underage student to come by, but they were also free most of the time. In my mind, as long as my academic achievement was high, I was free to drink and party as often as I desired.

These were fun times in many ways, due to the excitement, the newness, and the sheer daring of breaking campus rules and getting by with it. Yet there was within me an underlying insecurity, marked with emptiness, depression, and fear. When I started college, it had been several months since I started taking prescription anti-depressants. During the last few weeks of my senior year of high school, some faculty members noticed my depression. After urging my parents to take me to a psychiatrist, I met with a doctor who placed me on anti-depressant medication. But the daily pills had yet to help. In fact, the depression continued to worsen. Then, toward the middle of my freshman year in college, something very unusual took place. And I wasn't prepared for the struggles it would bring.

17

Chapter 5

Lithium, Lies, and Liquor

Melancholia is the beginning and a part of mania . . . . The development of a mania is really a worsening of the disease (melancholia) rather than a change into another disease.

ARETAEUS OF CAPPADOCIA (c. 30-90 AD)

Therefore the king said to me, "Why is your face sad, since you are not sick? This is nothing but sorrow of heart." So I became dreadfully afraid.

NEHEMIAH 2:2 NKJV

My roommate's alarm clock sounded loudly, forcing me to awaken abruptly. I knew it was back – I just didn't have an exact name for it. It was that strange entity that might be called a sense of dread, a black cloud, or simply an awareness of a dismal existence. It was a sense of foreboding that constantly lurked in the background, waiting for the right time to rear its ugly head, and to make this already challenging time in my life nearly overwhelming.

I was still in my freshman year of college when a series of bizarre changes began to take place. I went from the usual feelings of depression and hopelessness into a pattern of very distinct mood swings, which occurred at two-week intervals. While on a two-week

18

"high," I had an unusual amount of energy. My thought processes were heightened and I never grew tired. This was not an inconvenience since I was able to do all my chemistry homework in less than half the time it usually took. I was amazed at how clearly and quickly my mind worked. During these "highs" I became very talkative and outgoing, more so than ever before. I was somewhat hyperactive as a child and was often told to calm down, but this was an all-new experience for me.

After about two weeks, I would hit rock bottom, losing all of my energy and feeling it was impossible to even get out of bed. During my "high" periods I would hardly feel the need for sleep. But whenever I was going into one of my "lows," I would recognize it immediately when waking up in the morning. I could feel happy and energetic the night before, only to wake up with a total sense of doom. When I felt this hopelessness come upon me, it took everything I had to make it to class or to my part-time job on campus.

Eventually, this back-and-forth pendulum became more than I could handle. I continued taking the antidepressants that were prescribed to me, but they didn't help. I was drinking on the weekends and sometimes during the week, depending on what parties and events were taking place. However, my drinking was still not out of control—or so it seemed. I was still studying for many hours and was diligently driven toward success.

In the midst of this chaos, there were many times when thoughts of suicide would creep in and add to my helplessness. I had

19

experienced this type of thinking during high school, but now it was becoming more prominent. Hiding this was becoming more difficult. People were starting to notice that something wasn't right, and some felt the need to confront me.

During my sophomore year, one of my roommates closely witnessed the depression first hand. This young woman's family intervened in my situation and suggested I see a reputable psychiatrist in town. During my first appointment I was immediately diagnosed with atypical bipolar disorder, which is also referred to as manic depression.

The only option for treatment was a drug called lithium. The doctor prescribed four tablets a day and it was understood that I would be taking the drug for the rest of my life. In addition, I was prescribed other antidepressants and anti-anxiety drugs. I also had to be treated for thyroid problems due to the lithium causing an imbalance in my thyroid gland. During this time I was taking 10 to 14 prescription pills per day, and at times even more. I could easily persuade my doctor to write additional prescriptions for pain pills and sleeping pills to anesthetize myself from life.

After being on the medication for a while, I continued to have suicidal thoughts and depression. Contrary to doctor's orders, I continued to drink alcohol. I would later have another doctor tell me it was a miracle I had lived with all of the chemicals and alcohol in my system at once. Little did I know the road I was traveling would take me further than I ever wanted to go.

Chapter 6

Psych Ward Blues

Nothing can stop the man with the right mental attitude from achieving his goal; nothing on Earth can help the man with the wrong mental attitude.

THOMAS JEFFERSON

My days are over. My hopes have disappeared. My heart's desires are broken.

JOB 17:11 NLT

The tightly sealed security door that led to the psychiatric unit of St. Joseph's Hospital closed behind my two sisters and me. My doctor suggested hospitalization for my extreme depression, and my sisters were helping me through the hospital admission process. My younger sister was also a college student at the University of Kentucky, and lived in the same city as I. My older sister lived an hour away in Louisville, and she came to Lexington to be with me during this time. My parents were more than three hours away and couldn't come right away.

The hospital staff searched my bags for any objectionable or dangerous objects. I nearly cried when they took away my glass bottle of facial moisturizer—sharp objects, like glass, that could cut or injure the patient were not allowed. I was even more upset when they said I couldn't have my Walkman cassette player. They explained that the cord on the headphones could be used to harm myself. This was extremely upsetting, as music was the one thing besides alcohol that helped me cope with pain and loneliness—and they were taking that away.

I tried to remain strong and act like I was going to be okay. I wanted to keep it all together so I would not add any fuel to the fire that I had started. Although I was a mess, I felt the need to make sure that everyone around me was emotionally sound.

My sisters spent some time with me while I got settled, but they went home when visiting hours ended. They left me with a roommate I was not looking forward to knowing. For all I knew, she had more than one personality to get acquainted with. I had never been in this type of situation, and was really not sure what to expect or what was expected of me.

Putting a depressed person in the middle of other psychiatric cases is hardly a prescription for relieving depression. I was surrounded by people who had gone off the deep end. I heard horrible, maniacal screams as I lay in bed at night. Among my fellow patients was a young man who thought we were all caught in a time warp and that the year in which we were living was happening over and over again. He looked like a typical college guy from the late 80s, with a preppy, pink button-down shirt. He reminded me of someone I would meet in a bar, not a psychiatric unit. I also recall a short, red-haired woman who claimed to have the power of levitation.

I felt completely out of place, and yet I couldn't connect with anyone on the outside either. My life didn't make sense. I had gone from being a fairly happy, energetic, smart kid to someone who was completely powerless over her life. I almost wanted to shake myself and see if this was not all a long nightmare. What had gone wrong? How had I ended up in a place like this, locked behind security doors without any freedom to come and go as I pleased?

Of course, it was not against my own will that I checked into the hospital. Out of desperation I had agreed to the doctor's suggestion. After all, I had no other options on the horizon. And though I had willingly followed my doctor's orders, I never quite understood how my period of hospitalization was supposed to help me. The staff kept me behind locked doors, gave me medication, and had me attend a few group therapy sessions. No one talked with me one on one. The nurses stayed at a distance and treated all patients equally, which is to say they treated us like we were crazy.

Ironically, I had once been on the staff side of a psychiatric ward. During the first couple of summers after graduating from high school, I worked as an EKG technician in a large hospital in my hometown. I performed EKGs on patients all over the hospital. Quite often, I had to enter the hospital's psych ward to run EKGs on the patients there.

23

I remember one of my patients very well. She was a young woman in her early twenties. I can still remember being shocked at this woman who seemed out of her mind. She didn't look like a deranged lunatic, but rather like a model out of a fashion magazine. In bodily and facial appearance, she would have been the envy of any woman. What amazed me most was that someone so beautiful on the outside could be so messed up inside. Whether her problem was drug addiction or some other psychiatric condition, I don't know. What I do know is that I never imagined that in a year or so, I would be in a psychiatric ward again—this time as a patient.

Around the time of my first admittance to the psychiatric unit, I wasn't thinking about the long-term future. All of the medication made it impossible to think clearly and left me living in a fog with the goal of surviving moment by moment.

After being discharged from my first hospitalization, I continued with college and was fairly functional. I kept my grades up, but I continued to drink more and more. I also began to use recreational drugs. About a year later I was back in the psych ward. This time a counselor came to my room and asked about my drinking patterns. I knew all of the right things to say to convince her that drinking wasn't really a problem for me, although deep down I knew it was one of the main problems. Soon, I was discharged a second time and I continued with life as usual.

Before you get the picture that every waking hour of my life was a horrible nightmare, let me say that there were still some fun and exciting times during these years. I loved the freedom of being away from the fairly small town I grew up in. I was living in a larger city, with a lot more cultural options than I was accustomed to. I loved the unique shops in the university district. I loved being within walking distance of downtown, with its tall buildings and interesting architecture. I loved the city and its nightlife. I had always loved music, and Lexington had an impressive live music scene. Many of my evenings were spent listening to good music in the various bars and pubs. I also enjoyed meeting people from all walks of life. Eventually, my circle of acquaintances and friends would become more diverse than I could have imagined.

But before that happened, I gave my search for religious spirituality one more chance. After all, I had nothing to lose. Unfortunately, there wasn't much to gain either.

Chapter 7

Mail-Order Religion

That's me in the corner

That's me in the spotlight

Losing my religion.

R.E.M.

**For I say to you, that unless your righteousness exceeds the
righteousness of the scribes and Pharisees, you will by no means
enter the kingdom of heaven.**

JESUS IN MATTHEW 5:20 NKJV

Dan and I pulled a late night study session to prep for a big
chemistry test. We were young, ambitious, and determined to make a
good grade by any means possible. Having implemented every study
tool available, including large doses of caffeine, Dan had another idea
for ensuring a good grade. I was open to his suggestion.

He explained that some of his fellow high school graduates
happened to be Christians. They also happened to be students at the
university. He proposed that we ask them to pray for us. I don't
remember the words he used to convince me that we should visit
these particular young men in their dorm room, but I understood that

26

they might have some sort of direct connection to God and their prayers might be of value.

Dan had been raised religious like me, but I got the picture that the religion of his friends was different. I was willing to try anything for a good grade, so one evening we visited one of the men's dormitories on campus. I was introduced to a couple of guys, and Dan said he would go first. They sat Dan on a chair in the middle of the room, put their hands on his back and shoulders, and began asking for the blessings of God, particularly as it pertained to the upcoming chemistry exam.

It seemed a little strange, but I took a seat in the same chair after they prayed for Dan. I expected to feel differently afterwards, but nothing changed. All I felt was disappointment.

The experience in the dorm was yet another dry, dead spiritual let down. I had hoped these young students could, in some tangible way, demonstrate a true knowledge of God and a connection to that which is divine. Sure, I wanted to do well on my chemistry test, but my willingness to be prayed for had more to do with needing peace than wanting a good grade.

The situation discouraged me, but it didn't stop me from seeking God through religion for a little while. I occasionally attended mass at the Catholic Newman Center on campus, but that didn't last long.

College eventually caused me to question the validity of Christianity, but for a season I was open to what others had to say.

During freshman orientation, I had filled out a card signifying that I would like more information about a local Christian organization on campus. In full disclosure, I filled out the card so I would actually get some mail in my mailbox, even if it was only junk mail. I ended up getting more than mail. I got a phone call from an upperclassman on campus. She asked if she could come by my dorm room so we could meet. Being too nice to say no, I told her that would be fine.

She came by, we talked briefly, and she asked if we could meet in the student center for lunch. Not wanting to hurt her feelings, I reluctantly agreed.

When we got together, she gave me "The Four Spiritual Laws," an evangelistic tract used by Campus Crusade for Christ. She took me through the booklet page by page, but I could not even begin to grasp its meaning. It seemed completely irrelevant to my life.

This young lady's intentions were no doubt pure, and there may have been others who were changed in a positive way by the message of her booklet, but my heart was not in a condition to even begin to understand true reconciliation to God. So I did my best to politely get her to stop calling me.

Sometime after that, I attended a Bible study held by an older student who lived in my sorority house. Several of us met in her room or in the living room of the house. There was something different about this particular young woman. Whenever we had formal dances, she was one of the only people present not binging on booze, yet she seemed to have as much fun, if not more, than everyone else there.

Her Bible studies captured my attention for a while, but I eventually stopped attending. My focus was turning more and more toward where the next party was, or who would accompany me to a local bar, where I would use my fake ID to get in and get drunk.

At this point I was becoming more and more intrigued with the alternative downtown culture. I loved the music and the nightlife. There were so many varieties of people to meet and places to go. I wanted to experience it all.

Chapter 8

Radio Free Lexington

**There is no feeling, except the extremes of fear
and grief, that does not find relief in music.**
GEORGE ELIOT

**Begin the music, strike the timbrel, play the
melodious harp and lyre.**
PSALM 81:3 NIV

I walked into the offices for WRFL, Radio Free Lexington, and told the personnel there that I wanted to be an on-air DJ. I was just getting over a cold, and my speech was low and raspy. The young man who greeted me told me I had a really cool voice that would sound great on the radio. Unfortunately, I had to let him down by admitting it was only temporary. But in a short time, I was starting my DJ training.

The college radio station was an exciting place to be, with its enormous selection of every type of music imaginable. As a DJ for an independent station, I was able to play any music I selected, and I got a Friday night slot for my first time on air.

At one point, I began dating a member of the station crew. My first date with this young man, whom we will call Robert, proved very interesting. He later told me he had sold his entire CD collection in order to have money to take me to dinner. I felt pretty bad about it, but I was a little relieved that he'd been able to keep all of his autographed CDs.

When we got to the restaurant he chose, the waitress took our drink order. I, of course, ordered a beer. Robert ordered a soft drink and told me he didn't drink because he had to take a prescribed medication that wasn't supposed to mix with alcohol. When I asked him what he was taking, I was surprised to hear that he was also taking lithium to control his bipolar disorder. We had more in common than I first realized. We were both manic depression patients, yet he was the only one with sense enough to not mix alcohol with his prescribed pills. I never heeded the warnings of the doctor or of the labels on my prescription bottles.

My relationship with Robert didn't last long. I had no intention of getting too close to him—or anyone for that matter. I usually kept a few guys around, but never gave any of them too much attention. In fact, on one of my birthdays, Robert, as well as two other guys, seemed to be under the impression that they were each my date for the evening. In what was probably an awkward night for all of them, we spent time at a downtown rock club, listening to some local bands. I didn't end the night with any one of the three young men, but rather spent it in a drunken conversation with a guy I had never met before and never saw again.

It was the typical behavior of a selfish, self-absorbed alcoholic. As someone who had once been considerate of other people's feelings, I was quickly becoming someone who cared only about instant gratification. And I was incapable of having any type of meaningful relationship.

I started hanging out with musicians who also liked to drink and smoke marijuana. I later acquired a bass guitar and started jamming with friends who played in bands. Many of the people I hung out with tenaciously strived to be rock stars. I had one group of friends who had completely walked away from any normality in their lives. They lived in an old, run-down house without central heat or basic amenities, and spent all their time trying to make good music. Lots of people hung out during jam sessions, during which local musicians of all ages came and went, partaking in the music and the marijuana. I usually felt like one of the guys and always felt more at home hanging out with my guy friends than with a bunch of young college women.

It was a time of exploration. I was on a journey to know my true self. Without being able to put it into words, I wanted to know what my purpose was. I wanted to find true freedom. But I would only find freedom's counterfeits.

Chapter 9

"I'm Amy, and I'm an Alcoholic"

**First you take a drink, then the drink takes a drink, then the
drink takes you.**

F. SCOTT FITZGERALD

**Wine is a mocker, strong drink is a brawler, and whoever is led
astray by it is not wise.**

PROVERBS 20:1 NIV

I sat in the corner of an old basement room in downtown
Lexington, looking into a sea of faces black and white, young and old.
The building in which these strangers and I had gathered was in the
center of beautiful and historic Gratz Park. We entered the old stone
structure by descending a crumbling set of outdoor stairs. Inside,
individuals took turns verbally sharing situations in their lives. Each
began with the phrase, "Hi, I'm so and so…, and I'm an alcoholic,"
before talking about problems with spouses, money, job situations,
and everything in between.

I had been seeing a counselor in addition to my regular visits
to the psychiatrist. My counselor finally convinced me to attend an
Alcoholics Anonymous meeting. She had a friend who was willing to
meet me at a given location so we could go to the meeting together. I

eventually agreed, and I still remember what I wore to the meeting—a royal blue sweater. The color suited my complexion, especially since my hair was dyed jet black. With determination to look good, I wanted to convince all in attendance that I didn't have a problem. I went to the AA gathering as an observer and was pleased when the meeting was over and I got away without anyone prying into my life.

I didn't attend another AA meeting for some time, but later I started going to meetings off and on, as it was becoming clear to me that I needed some help. I began to regularly attend one particular AA group geared towards college students. The meetings were held in a building right next to the university campus. In those meetings, poker chips were given out to signify lengths of sobriety. Whoever led the meeting would ask if anyone needed a white, red, or blue chip. A white chip meant someone had acquired 24 hours of sobriety or had a desire to stop drinking, and I received my fair share of white chips. Blue chips symbolized one month of sobriety. Red chips were given for six months without a drink.

I can still remember a young woman standing up one evening to receive a red chip. I was amazed. I could not believe that someone could actually go for six months without a drink of liquor. I couldn't make it for a single month, much less six. In my mind it would be impossible to stay sober for that long, but I was willing to try. Unfortunately, I ended up in a drug and alcohol rehabilitation program before I ever succeeded. Not only was my drinking getting way out of hand, but so was my behavior.

On one occasion I was asked to attend a fraternity dance with a young man I didn't know very well. All the guys were in tuxedos, and all of the women were in formal dresses. Dinner was first, and the dance would be held in another section of the same ballroom.

I was extremely drunk before we even began to eat. After dinner, my date and I went to our hotel room, which we were sharing with at least one other couple. I decided to get comfortable, so I changed into shorts and a T-shirt. The dance had not even begun.

My date was upset and embarrassed that his date showed up on the dance floor wearing casual clothing while everyone else was in formal attire. I don't remember much about the evening after that.

Sometime later, I went for my third stay at St. Joseph's Hospital. Unlike the first two times, I was now placed in the chemical dependency unit. While in rehabilitation I received shots of Phenobarbital to assist in withdrawing from the alcohol. At this point, I had become a daily drinker. I would usually have a few drinks before my morning classes. I had even been daring enough to sit in my college English class with a cup of bourbon and Coke in my hand. To finish the day of drinking, I passed out from drunkenness nearly every night.

My body craved alcohol when it didn't have it. I felt like I was at the end of my rope, and I didn't want to live with an alcohol addiction and all of the strange behaviors that accompany such a lifestyle. I was tired of going into a panic every time I ran out of whiskey.

35

I still remember the night one of my drinking buddies took the last swig out of a bottle of bourbon. It was late, and all the bars and liquor stores were closed. I went into a panic-filled rage, because I knew I would have to survive the rest of the night without another drink. I was infuriated with my friend as I watched him turn up the bottle and finish it off. I remember thinking he should have been more considerate of my needs, even though he was probably the one who purchased the liquor.

While in rehab, I had several days to sober up and start thinking without the influence of hard liquor. I was determined to be finished with drinking. After a few days, I got used to rehab culture. Nearly everyone there was a chain smoker. Cigarettes seemed the most common coping mechanism among rehab patients as they went through withdrawals, so I fell right into the crowd and began chain smoking as well. We all reasoned that if we were no longer going to do drugs or drink liquor, we at least had our cigarettes to enjoy. I was still bent on bodily destruction, yet a part of me was desperately striving for a life of wholeness.

Now that I had been sober for a short time, I had no intention of going back to the life I lived before rehab. My senior year of college was nearing, and I'd gone from making nearly all A's every semester to practically failing one of my science courses.

This was a wake-up call, or at least it should have been. I knew I had hurt my parents, even though I never intended to. In my mind I was going to stay sober this time! I really intended to start a new life in which substance abuse had no part. I had a lot of time to get the liquor out of my system while in rehab, and I had a lot of time to think. I was ready to get on with my life, whatever that meant.

Eventually the time came to leave the rehabilitation center. Fear gripped me as I stood at the doors of the facility, preparing to face the outside world without any substance to numb the pain or to ease my anxiety. This time I would not have my "crutch" or my "fix." Nevertheless, I told myself that I was going to make it as a sober citizen.

I did make it – for about a week.

Chapter 10

Off the Wagon

I have very poor and unhappy brains for drinking. I could well wish courtesy would invent some other custom of entertainment.
WILLIAM SHAKESPEARE IN *OTHELLO*
For the gate is wide and the way is easy that leads to destruction, and those who enter by it are many.
MATTHEW 7:13 ESV

To this day I still don't recall obtaining the bourbon that took me down that destructive path again. I suppose I purchased it from a local liquor store. The only part of my drunken rendezvous that I remember is walking alone in a park in the middle of the day with a bottle of bourbon, concealed by a brown paper bag. Later that day I somehow made it back to the sorority house where I was living, but I had lost my car. Julie, one of my closest friends, realized I was extremely drunk and became very angry with me, asking how I could do such a thing. I found it ironic since she had been one of my biggest drinking buddies before my stint in rehab. Even she was becoming irritated at my behavior.

Julie and I had shared some extremely wild and fun times together. She was always game for an adventure, and sometimes our escapades put us in danger of getting into some sticky situations. Our adventures included zipping through Matamoras, Mexico, in an old taxi bus during spring break.

On another occasion, we took a trip to New York City along with two other sorority sisters. We went to a Manhattan nightclub where the booze was flowing freely. Julie and I climbed on top of the bar where drinks were being served and began to dance. New Yorkers apparently found it humorous to watch young, drunk women from Kentucky act ridiculous. At one point while dancing on the bar, I looked away from Julie, and when I looked back, she was no longer on top of the bar. She'd fallen backwards and miraculously avoided colliding with any drinking glasses or bottles of liquor.

Another one of our antics involved breaking into the fine arts building on campus in the middle of the night. We went into the theater, cranked up all of the lights and put on our own show. When we were finished, we took an office chair from the building. The chair was on wheels and we sat in it as we rolled down Rose Street in the dark.

Once we got into a car with a stranger. He had a lot of cash and was buying drinks for everyone at a bar close to campus. We arrived at a large house and went inside. It was filled with people we had never seen before. Julie and I were both drunk and paranoid and wondered if we had been kidnapped. We began sneaking around inside the house, looking for a telephone book so we could call a cab.

Thankfully, we had not been kidnapped. We just did not have enough clarity of mind to know why we had ended up in a strange house with strange people. I still don't recall how we got home, but somehow we got away from there.

Julie always seemed wildly uncontrollable, but I was the one who couldn't stop drinking. Now that I was on that destructive path again, there was no turning back. I had fallen off the wagon, and once that happens to a person with that type of addiction, it's hard to get back on. The insanity of alcoholism is that at one moment, a person can be absolutely convinced that he or she is finished with drinking. But once the alcohol is re-introduced into the body's system, all thoughts of staying sober are out the door and the quest is on to get more to drink.

Alcoholism had its grip on me, and I knew that I was going to have to find a different crowd to hang with—one that was just as serious about drinking as I was. Most of the young women who lived in the sorority house with me drank at parties, but they were not in my league. They wouldn't tolerate my destructiveness, so I would find some serious drinkers who would.

I had already started to hang around the "alternative" crowd and had been a part of the rock and punk music scene. I spent many nights at bars and music clubs, meeting people who loved to party and listen to music as much as I did. After drinking at a nearby bar, my new friends and I would usually listen to one of the local rock bands at a music club. When the bars closed at 1 a.m., we would hit the dance clubs, which stayed open another three hours. At these clubs I became exposed to people from all walks of life. There were punk rockers with their multi-colored four inch high Mohawks; gothics with all-black attire, white-painted faces, and black lip stick; and transvestites with fur coats and feather boas. There was so much variety, and I loved the excitement. Yet, looking back, it is remarkable to think that all of those people were on a search as well, trying to find their place and purpose in this world.

It has always been in my nature to go against the norms of culture, at least to some degree. Even before going into rehab, I had already rebelled against the social norms of sorority life, which is quite conservative. I dressed in more "alternative" clothing, wearing wild-patterned shirts and skirts, and a black leather biker's jacket. I upset some of my sorority sisters when I hung an old hippie-looking curtain out my sorority house bedroom window, possibly upsetting everyone on sorority row. When my drinking became severe, I began to hang out with drug users and dealers, often sleeping on people's couches rather than returning to the scrutiny of my roommates. I went wherever my habits were welcomed and duplicated.

As long as there were people to enable my lifestyle, I would continue to live it. It would take hitting rock bottom for me to stop. Sometimes we have to be flat on our backs at the bottom of the barrel, looking up. For me, I would have to reach a point where I had absolutely no one to turn to. As long as people would support me

41

financially and in other ways, I would continue down the path of destruction.

Chapter 11

Unproductive Therapy

No psychologist should pretend to understand what he does not understand... Only fools and charlatans know everything and understand nothing.

ANTON CHEKHOV

Do not gaze at wine when it is red, when it sparkles in the cup, when it goes down smoothly! In the end it bites like a snake and poisons like a viper. Your eyes will see strange sights and your mind imagine confusing things.

PROVERBS 21:31-33 NIV

I parked my little red Buick in the cramped parking lot behind an old remodeled building near the university. It was time for my weekly group therapy session with my two group counselors. One was a yuppie-looking man with a full beard, probably in his mid to late forties. The other was a fashionable, yet smart-looking woman in her fifties.

I entered the group therapy room and sat quietly, waiting for the other clients to arrive. My presence was the result of my psychiatrist's recommendation. I wondered if he had any clue what took place in the meetings.

Eventually the other members of the group gathered, and our two counselors joined us. It was time for "open discussion." No one was required to talk, and I never said much. I was too withdrawn to share anything. Plus, I didn't see how these talking sessions (which my parents were shelling out lots of money for) could really help. I usually sat and listened to the others, wondering if our two leaders were ever going to offer any solutions. They never did.

What they did was allow extremely dysfunctional individuals to regurgitate their strange thoughts and actions from the previous week. One woman was dating a man from the Middle East who insisted on controlling her every move. She was young, energetic, and athletic, but apparently too insecure to break off a relationship with someone who was both verbally and physically abusive. Every week I listened to her insanity, wondering what in the world it had to do with me and my inability to stop drinking.

At the time I was partly on the wagon, but mostly off. I would try to stop drinking for a little while, but it never lasted. But I never let those in the group therapy session in on the fact that I wasn't staying sober. I usually put up a good front—or at least I thought I did.

On one particular day, the female counselor confronted me before the group meeting. She insisted that she knew I was still drinking. I, of course, denied it with a list of lies.

Sometime after this event, she came into the restaurant where I was waiting tables. It was a popular local bar and restaurant with low lighting, an old jukebox that played classic hits, and seating sections with sofas for seats and antique trunks for tables. Needless to say, it was a hard place to work and stay sober. I was serving drinks, night after night, to people who appeared to be having a good time. Somehow I managed to stay sober for part of the time I worked there, but I eventually gave into the temptation and ordered a drink at closing time one evening. That night, I got extremely drunk and had to be carried to the apartment of one of my co-workers.

The night my group therapist came in was during one of those periods when I was trying to stay sober. She was not seated in my section, so I didn't have to wait on her. But I watched her as she sat with a couple of other women. I glared at her as she was served a mixed drink from the bar. Every time I walked past her table and eyed the drink in front of her, it made me angry—angry that she could drink and keep her composure, but I could not. Angry that she confronted me about my alcohol intake, yet she could casually sit with friends and have a drink and maintain her professionalism and dignity. I detested her.

I continued with the group sessions for a while longer. I don't remember why I stopped going, or even the time frame I was there, but I do recall that my involvement with the group session was another blow to my spirit. Being surrounded by others who were seemingly hopeless did nothing to bolster my outlook on life. It only brought me down further.

Chapter 12

Out of Control

**No passion so effectually robs the mind of all its powers of
acting and reasoning as fear.**

> **EDMUND BURKE IN *THE SUBLIME AND
> BEAUTIFUL***

**A man who isolates himself seeks his own desire; He rages
against all wise judgment.**

> **PROVERBS 18:1 NKJV**

I was lying on the hallway floor of my shared apartment. I was
no longer the All-American girl. I wasn't even the semi-coping
sorority sister. I was more like Elizabeth Taylor in the movie *Who's
Afraid of Virginia Woolf*, throwing a pouting, alcoholic fit mixed with
an alarming cry of desperation. I would often go into hysterical rages,
throwing and kicking whatever was in the way. I had the appearance
of death with a malnourished, uncared-for body and gothic rock attire
that included black lipstick, jet-black hair, a black leather jacket and
fishnet stockings. I still remember the words of my roommate, who
had so graciously tolerated me up until this point. He said I was
pathetic, and he was through trying to help me. My closest drinking

partner for quite some time, he was the last person left in my life, and now he was threatening to walk out on my extreme dysfunction.

My roommate Dan (the same Dan from a previous chapter) had been my friend for several years and my enabler for the last two. He came from a very affluent family, so as his roommate, I got to drink excessively and in style. We ate and drank in restaurants and bars every day and traveled at will. It was wonderful in some ways. But just as success and popularity had never made me happy, I was discovering money could not make me happy either.

Dan would have bought me anything I wanted. He took care of my bills, the rent, and the entertainment. He was generous and smart, graduating at the top of his college class. But I was not looking for success, popularity, money, or fame. I was looking for peace.

One of the things that drew Dan and me together was our love for music. We spent countless hours listening to local bands and traveling to concerts in central Kentucky and southern Ohio. From Louisville to Cincinnati to Dayton, we stopped at nothing to see our favorite acts play live on stage.

Together, we saw all my favorite bands. I was highly inspired by the women bass players who emerged during the late 80s and early 90s. In fact, I had wanted to be a musician since I was about five years old. Music was the one element of life that had the ability to ease my often-troubled soul. When I was listening to well-played live music, I could forget my worries and cares, at least temporarily.

Dan and I eventually bought our own instruments. I took a few lessons from a local musician who said I was a natural at the bass. It was certainly the right fit, since I had always kept my eyes on the hands of the bass player, no matter what band I was watching. After that, Dan and I would get together with friends for jam sessions. Our love for music was definitely a major factor in our relationship.

But the main reason Dan and I were drawn to one another was that he was searching for peace, too. We were on a journey together. We would often drive in his car for hours, looking for something we could not put our fingers on. Whatever that something was, we never found it. We continued our journey together until I surpassed him in insanity. Although he tried to help me find peace, he didn't have the answers either.

Occasionally we stopped at Matthew's Garden, a special conservatory on campus. The garden of plants and trees was surrounded by a white fence, and we would park his car close by and stand against the garden's outer barrier. On one occasion, as we stood by the fence, we felt an unusual breeze sweep by. As it did, tears welled up in my eyes. I turned to Dan and saw similar tears in his eyes. He turned and asked me, "Did you feel that?" We both felt a sense of peace come over us, a peace that seemed "other worldly," an experience I'd never had before.

The biblical name Matthew means gift. Its literal meaning is "gift of Jehovah." It seems God Himself visited us with the undeserved gift of His presence at Matthew's Garden. I still wonder if

49

He was trying to get our attention and demonstrate His love for us, even though we were a long way from knowing Him.

There had been other times during those years when God's love was demonstrated to me through simple occurrences in nature. The summer after my sophomore year in college, I worked on a university research farm where we cross-pollinated corn for genetic study. I had grown up in the suburbs, but I felt at home with farm labor. I loved being close to nature and the rich soil of the farm. Every night that summer, I partied hard with my friends. But every morning, I faithfully walked from my apartment to campus and rode with our crew to the farm in one of the campus vans.

One hot, sunny day, we were taking a break and I sat alone next to a tree, wondering if there was a God. That instant, a Monarch butterfly landed on my leg and stayed for some time while I observed its beauty. I was amazed that it did not fly away immediately, but lingered as though a familiar friend. Even then I felt God Himself was answering my question about His existence with this small sign.

On another occasion, I went camping deep in the woods with some friends. I was trying to stay clean and sober at the time and became very upset when some people I was with started smoking marijuana around the campfire one night. I didn't want to give in to the temptation, so I wandered alone through the woods in the dark until I came to a secluded pond and sat on its small dock. Sitting there alone and shaken, I was amazed to see a shooting star zip through the sky right above me. It was an amazing sight on that clear, hot summer night. I had always wanted to see a shooting star, but never had the opportunity. And that night, in my despair, a beautiful flash of light held my gaze, if only for a few glorious seconds.

A short time later, another camper came looking for me and sat next to me on the dock. Out of the blue, she asked me if I believed in God. It was as though God in His goodness was showing me that He was out there and that He cared for me.

But through the years the darkness in my life would eventually trump the small, yet profound signs of God's presence. Those occurrences were eventually overshadowed and forgotten, but the search for peace continued.

A couple years later, the subject of God came up again while Dan and I were drinking beer in the dark corner of a bar. We had both already had a few, so I was not amused when Dan began to tell me that he felt like God had placed him on Earth to carry out a powerful mission. I sat dumbfounded as I listened to what I thought was a ridiculous notion. In reality, he was trying to bear his soul to me and I laughed in his face and told him he was an arrogant fool. All that I could see when I looked at us were two lost individuals feeding their carnal nature with booze day after day.

Angry, I turned to him and said, "How dare you think that you are somebody special in God's eyes, if there even is a God! Just who do you think you are?" Because *I* felt so low and useless, I couldn't let Dan think he might have some divine purpose for being on Earth. I hurt his feelings, but I couldn't see past our destructive behavior. I saw no purpose other than living for the next moment with as little pain as possible. I couldn't fathom the thought that Dan might be someone special when I felt so useless and inadequate.

The truth is that Dan had a real heart of compassion, and I had seen him reach out to homeless people and other hurting individuals on several occasions. I now realize that a deep care for others was a part of his nature.

About a year later, I was discussing the subject of God once again with a view that had shifted even more. Dan and I sat in a coffee house in the French Quarter of New Orleans, a city we visited on more than one occasion, always staying on Bourbon Street to be in the midst of the excitement that's part of that historic city. Where else do bars stay open with live music playing until 6 a.m.? It was a likely stop for us.

While sipping on some coffee, Dan asked if I believed in Heaven or Hell, angels or demons, God or the devil. My conclusion was that there may or may not be a God, but certainly demons, Hell, and the devil were myths. I scorned those who believed in such nonsense. By not believing in any of those forces of good and evil, I was convinced I wouldn't have to answer for anything I did or said. As far as I was concerned, I was free to live my life without anyone telling me what to do.

Chapter 13

Looking for a Way of Escape

It is difficult to free fools from the chains they revere.

VOLTAIRE

Be sober-minded; be watchful. Your adversary the devil prowls around like a roaring lion, seeking someone to devour.

1 PETER 5:8 ESV

A short time after the fit of rage described in the last chapter, I sat in my psychiatrist's office and relayed my out-of-control drinking situation to him. He suggested rehabilitation once again, and I agreed out of desperation.

I went home to pack my clothes against my doctor's suggestion. He wanted me to go straight to the hospital, but I lied and said I had no one to bring any of my belongings to me at the hospital. I had every intention of going to rehab, but I had one more thing I wanted to do.

When I got to the apartment I shared with Dan, I suggested he and I go across the street to a restaurant and bar where we had spent many, many hours. It was early in the evening—"happy hour."

Ironically, "happy hour" never made me very happy, but this occasion was a little different. Dan and I shared one last round of drinks. I then said to him, "By the way, can you drop me off at rehab in a little while?" I hadn't told him where I was going until I was in the middle of one last round.

I knew that would be the last drink. I still remember the date: November 19, 1992. Dan graciously agreed to call my parents to let them know where I was. As you can imagine, my relationship with them was a little strained. They didn't exactly know how to handle me, and as is the case with most alcoholics, I did what I wanted no matter what anyone suggested.

After going to the rehabilitation clinic, I continued with an outpatient program where I got to know a lot of the other patients. I made some changes in my way of living and got my own apartment so I could get away from temptation. I stopped hanging around my old crowd and the familiar hang-outs. I found support and stayed sober. Believe it or not, I was close to graduating from college and was going to do it sober.

Because I had lived day to day on prescription drugs and alcohol, I had lost my perception of time and was nearly in shock when my advisor told me I only had one more semester of classes to take until I graduated. I had thought I was only a sophomore or junior. It is embarrassing to realize how clueless I was about my own life.

I still have trouble recollecting much of what happened during those years. Looking at pictures at my mother's house a few years ago, I saw a photograph of me standing next to a young gentleman with his arm around me. He was wearing a tuxedo and black tie, I was wearing a formal dress, and I had no recollection of ever having seen him. My mom and sisters assured me that he had been my date to a formal sorority dance. Our sorority dances were always major events that usually took place out of town, so it's likely that I went to the dance, traveled out of town, and stayed overnight in a hotel with this guy I couldn't remember. To this day, I cannot recall the event.

On another occasion, my older sister came to stay in my dorm with me for about a week. A few years ago, when she mentioned her visit and some of the places we'd gone when she came, I couldn't recollect the event even occurring.

But I finally entered into a time of sobriety. I would like to say this was the beginning of great and wonderful things. Unfortunately, this was not the case. Some good things did take place and at least I was no longer in the danger I faced before. With sobriety, I could look back and say I was truly grateful to be alive. But with sobriety there was also a great price to pay, one that would eventually cause me to lose my mind.

Chapter 14

Getting With the Program

Physicians who are familiar with alcoholism agree there is no such thing as making a normal drinker out of an alcoholic.

ALCOHOLICS ANONYMOUS, *THE BIG BOOK*

Keep me from lying to myself; give me the privilege of knowing your instructions.

PSALM 119:29 NLT

It was Thanksgiving. My new friend Louise and I had just been released from a drug and alcohol rehabilitation clinic and were enrolled in an outpatient program. Louise was at least thirty years my senior. She had been in and out of programs for years with no immediate family, so we spent some time together, going to meetings and going to restaurants. We decided to attend a candle-lit Alcoholics Anonymous meeting on Thanksgiving evening. Neither of us had been sober long, so we remained silent and listened to some of the sober-living veterans. It was there that I first met Susan. She was leading the meeting with an air of sophistication that was unusual for such gatherings. Although her clothes were dated, her overall persona was that of a refined and cultured woman.

I learned that Susan was a retired medical doctor who had been sober for an amazing ten years. I couldn't imagine staying sober for a decade. In my mind, she was the person who had all the answers I needed.

AA meetings became my new addiction. I was repeatedly told that I was an alcoholic and that I would always be an alcoholic. I was told that working the 12-step program of Alcoholics Anonymous was the only way to stay sober, and that it would be a lifetime process. I adopted these ideas and was determined to attend meetings for the rest of my life if necessary. I even got defensive if someone suggested I could stay sober without the meetings and the program.

One of the meetings I attended regularly was a Friday night women's group. Susan also attended this meeting and it was there that I got to know her. She and I, along with several other women, went to a restaurant every Friday evening after the meeting was over. Eventually, Susan invited me to her house. She freely offered guidance and counsel to anyone who would listen.

I was intrigued with everything she had to say. While educated in the medical field, she was very knowledgeable about history, world events, literature, and other subjects. I became extremely hungry for the knowledge that she had. I always had a strong desire for learning, but this hunger began to move beyond a simple interest in general knowledge.

Susan also spoke of many "spiritual" things. She emphasized that a spiritual experience was necessary in overcoming drug and

57

alcohol addiction, which I still believe to this day. But her brand of spirituality was unconventional to say the least. Initially, she claimed to be able to tap into spiritual realms that others weren't in tune with. She also claimed to gain enlightenment through channeling information through the spirit realm. Later, her claims became even more outrageous.

The first time I ate dinner at her house, Susan told me it was my job to make the salad. Some of the other women present chuckled and said, "Yeah, the newcomer always makes the salad." This didn't seem significant at first, but I now know that I was one of countless young women to fall into Susan's game. Anyone who didn't concede to what Susan said was either ousted from the group or became wise to Susan's manipulation and left on her own accord. Either way, Susan was in control. Having me make the salad was her way of getting me broken in to other things to come.

She had a way of pulling people into her "family" and making them feel at home. This was the perfect bait for young, insecure women in AA who had already wrecked their lives in so many ways. Inviting people into her nice home was the perfect way for her to take control of their thinking and eventually their actions.

Without realizing it, I was becoming one of her cult followers. Over time, the things she discussed became more and more bizarre, but I still believed she was truly enlightened, as I listened to her claim to have special insight into both historical and current events.

Looking back, I know that a lot of her theories were the same spread by occultists and even neo-Nazis. Of course, she never used the word Nazi or occult. She had her own code language. And yet she was very open about her strange political leanings and prejudices, which were extremely anti-Semitic and full of paranoia.

Ironically, I was living a double life once again, much like I had done in high school. Most of my social circle consisted of friends and roommates who had no idea what I was involved in when I would go to meet with Susan and her followers.

During this period of time, I lived with three roommates I met after becoming sober. Although one of them was prone to illegal drug use, none were frequent drinkers, and so our rented house was a safe haven from the drinking world. My three roommates were all artists who spent more time drinking coffee and working on art projects than going out and partying. In fact, we lived directly across the street from a very popular coffee house, which was like our second home. I was in graduate school at this time, and I spent many hours at the coffee house doing my homework.

My roommates opened up a whole new world for me. It was from these three individuals that I learned a lot about being free from the pressures and constraints of conformity. These were three individuals who taught me that it's okay to be different from the mainstream. They taught me how to be daring and how to let go of all of society's pressures to conform. Much of their philosophy is still relevant to me today.

However, much of the freedom I learned during this time in my life was a false type of freedom, driven by the spirit of a fallen world. The philosophy of those around me, as well as my own, was typical of the society in which we are now living. Ours was an attitude that said, "It is okay for me to do whatever I want to do, as long as it doesn't hurt anyone." I could justify any action I fancied at the moment,—the perfect environment in which the darkness of my soul was able to spread and eventually take over.

Chapter 15

Gay Until Graduation

The hunger for love is much more difficult to remove than the
hunger for bread.

MOTHER TERESA

That is why God abandoned them to their shameful desires.
Even the women turned against the natural way to have sex and
instead indulged in sex with each other.

ROMANS 1:26 NLT

My friend Erica took me to meet a woman named Beth, who
was working in a bread shop. It was a classic lesbian hookup. A
mutual friend of Erica and Beth had arranged for the two to meet after
Beth had divorced her husband to pursue a lesbian relationship.
Apparently Beth and Erica hit it off quickly, because within a few
short months, I attended the wedding ceremony for this newly formed
couple. The wedding, although not legally binding, took place in a
Unitarian church among a large group of friends and family. Even
Beth's ex-husband was in attendance.

Since third grade, I had wrestled with feelings of same-sex
attraction. I knew that my feelings were not the norm, so I suppressed
them for a long time. But during college, same-sex attraction became

even stronger, and I began to embrace thoughts that I would have done my best to conquer at one time.

The city I lived in lent itself to this ease of transition in my thought life. It was a city with a very high homosexual population where being gay was considered cool. There were even jokes among college students about being "gay until graduation." In other words, so many people experimented with living a homosexual lifestyle that it was considered normal in many people's eyes, even for that time period (the early 90s). Gay experimentation was encouraged within the university system and in courses that I took, such as Women's Literature, which exuded the idea that you were a tyrannical oppressor if you were not homosexual.

It was during the period that I lived with Dan that I began to venture into the gay culture. Homosexual nightlife was extremely prevalent in our city, with its many gay clubs and bars, where even prominent city officials could be seen watching drag shows or just hanging out having drinks. I even attended sessions with a counselor from the university's psychology department who tried to convince me that I must be a lesbian and that if I would stop suppressing it, I would finally be happy.

Many of my gay friends were fun to hang out with, and some were caring people who looked out for one another. But among many of them, there was a harshness and bitterness to their personalities, which I began to adopt. Most of us lived with a continual mission to justify our behavior and to have everyone in the world accept it. We relentlessly preached tolerance, but were actually intolerant of anyone whose views veered from our own. We were militant and miserable.

I found myself doing things and proclaiming things that I never thought I would be a part of. I began hanging out with people who were politically radical. A friend of mine led one of the main local activist groups that demanded equal rights for homosexuals, so I began participating in political activism as well.

I kept trying to find fulfillment during those years, but it was beyond my grasp. Many of the people I was in contact with were more messed up than I was, and none of them brought me joy or peace.

My own loneliness and darkness of soul had set me into the pursuit of dating women. But through those experiences I simply discovered more lonely individuals who were often more hate-filled and miserable than I was.

Special note: I want to make something clear here. As a Christian, I do not hate homosexuals, nor do I fear them. Therefore, I am not homophobic. I love homosexuals. Every same-sex attracted person is a special individual, created and deeply loved by God. In fact, there are times when I see someone living a gay lifestyle and I want to run to them, wrap my arms around them, and tell them how much they are loved by their Creator.

But I could also list a host of scriptural, psychological, and practical reasons that homosexuality is a lifestyle that runs counter to

God's design for our lives. I don't have the space in this book to do so, but the evidence is clear, and I have witnessed the negative consequences of homosexuality many times in my life.

Chapter 16

Darkness of Soul

Darkness was everywhere, it smelled like a tomb.

BOB DYLAN

Let no one be found among you who... practices divination or sorcery, interprets omens, engages in witchcraft, or casts spells, or who is a medium or spiritist or who consults the dead.

DEUTERONOMY 18:10-11 NIV

In a frantic rage, I drove my little red Buick around a downtown curve and pulled up to my friend Gwen's house. I was hoping to not see a black hearse driven by a particularly dark individual, and to my relief, the hearse was not there. The hearse belonged to one of Gwen's male friends whose preoccupation with death was so predominate even his vehicle was a symbol of death and darkness. He was the competition.

Gwen was my latest love interest, if the word love can be used here. Obsession is a more suitable word choice. Gwen demonstrated interest in me during her experimental adventure as a bisexual. She was not only interested in me, but also in a host of young men. Being powerfully manipulative, she had a way of pulling many of us into her game. She was the lead singer of a successful local rock band that had gained some national recognition in the college music scene, and she used her popularity and strong personality to cause everyone under her influence to do her bidding. Although she put on an air of confidence and arrogance, she was ruled by fear and insecurity.

On this particular evening, I was determined to be her sole interest, but it didn't work out that way. I entered her shared house and went upstairs to her room only to find more competition. This time my opponent was a small-framed, intelligent radio DJ, the latest member in her circle of influence. When Gwen saw me, she acted like I wasn't even there, despite her interest in me having been intense at one time. Now she was onto another pursuit, and it made me rage with anger. Somehow, I didn't let it show until I got back into my car alone.

My anger was amplified, as I had sacrificed more of my soul to spend time with Gwen. In the floor of the living room of her home was a pentagram in honor of Satan. Throughout the house were various symbols of religious blasphemy, including an upside-down cross above her bed. Her bedroom walls were lined with pages of the Bible, symbolizing disrespect for that which is sacred to so many.

She shared the house with other members of her band, all of whom probably thought the blasphemy and symbols of Satanism were humorous. I don't think anyone in that circle of friends regarded the Satanic worship as anything more than an amusing experiment;

however, there existed a form of mental assent toward evil, and I sensed it heavily that particular night when I went to her house alone.

I was so angry and hurt by her rejection. Yet I should not have been surprised. I'd seen her at work before and knew how she drew people into her circle of influence. But because of temporary blindness, I was quickly becoming the next casualty in her destructive operation.

I was becoming obsessive about relationships. I had already been deeply hurt by another woman, a college math instructor I met through my friend Erica. Her name was Josie, and I hoped my relationship with her would be lasting and meaningful, but she was just experimenting with her sexuality. Among some of her old friends, she kept our relationship a secret. I became hurt and offended by her desire for secrecy, because I was not only looking for love. I was looking for validity, to be accepted and justified in my choices.

But I was no different than Josie. I was experimenting as well, with one relationship after another. And now my experimenting was taking me to levels that were mentally and spiritually precarious. After my relationship with Josie fell apart, I continued looking for love in all the wrong places.

My relationship with Gwen was the beginning of my dabbling in witchcraft and the occult. In the subculture of which I was a part, there was a lot of interest in various forms of spirituality. I had one friend who was obsessed with vampires and began to dress like one and hang out with other "vampires." I had another friend who introduced me to Scientology, and I began to read the related literature and apply the teachings to my life. I also had an acquaintance who was a witch and I attended one of her parties along with her other witch friends.

The occult practices would later go deeper, as my mind was becoming more and more filled with dark thoughts. I tried to convince myself that I would somehow find peace. I thought that if I could just find the right people or the right philosophy, then everything would work out. I was on a desperate and frantic attempt to make it work. But the harder I tried, the more frustrated I became.

After I left Gwen's house that night, I wanted to let someone know how much I was hurting. I wanted revenge. I wanted to hurt those who had hurt me. I wanted to inflict pain on someone so that they would hurt as much as I did. Yet I did not even have enough courage to speak up for myself. I was a coward. And I was all alone.

Chapter 17

Under the Hypnotic Eye

The most terrible poverty is loneliness and the feeling of being unloved.

MOTHER THERESA

I lie awake, lonely as a solitary bird on the roof.

PSALM 102:7 NIV

I was shocked when a relative walked into my place of employment. He had come to Lexington for job training and stepped into the Hypnotic Eye Newsstand to buy some soft drinks and snacks. His presence jarred me into the reality of my hedonism. Surrounding me at the cash register was every variety of pornography, including some that was very hardcore.

It was a friend's shop, and we sold newspapers, periodicals, and magazines and served as a makeshift convenience store next to the university campus. It was my job to open the newsstand every morning of the week. Students, professors, and those who lived in the neighborhood walked past the shop every day, where I sold pornography to one of my graduate school professors on occasion.

I was an adamant supporter of equal rights for women, yet, hypocritically, I sold images of women's bodies for the gratification

69

of lust-ridden men. I didn't believe that treating women as sex objects was right, yet I was willing to sell porn in the name of free speech and free expression. It was hypocrisy at its worst.

Several of my friends who worked at the Hypnotic Eye also claimed to be advocates of free expression. We justified what we sold by referring to the fact that we made a wide variety of publications available to the public, not just pornography. However, much of the free expression we were selling exploited slaves of the porn industry. Our false idea of freedom contributed to the enslavement of others. Men who were slaves to their own sin were our regular customers, and we helped to perpetuate their addiction.

I remember the shame I felt when my cousin stood before me in that very seedy place. For a brief moment, I was unable to cover up my lowliness of existence, and I had to face the reality of it. Relief overwhelmed me when he finished purchasing his snacks and said goodbye, allowing me to go back to justifying my way of life.

The irony here is that a part of me really cared about the people in our neighborhood and those who shopped in the store. Some of my friends used to tease me because I was kind and friendly to customers. In our subculture, it was not considered cool to be overly kind or friendly. But the part of me that cared for others never died out completely, even though I was surrounded by a culture that frowned upon it.

During those years, I was rarely in the presence of children or the elderly, yet I longed to be near them. My interactions were with people from the university or with other people my own age who shared a similar lifestyle. I rarely visited family, and I never spent time with anyone outside of my own peer group.

My apartment was on a street that connected the campus to downtown. There was an elementary school on the street, and I would sometimes watch the kids as I walked by. They seemed so foreign to me. Once, a ball from the playground rolled into the street. I was overjoyed as I ran to get the ball and throw it back to a little boy who was chasing after it.

I believe I was drawn to children because I longed for a return to innocence. I longed to be free from the darkness that plagued my soul. I longed to run and skip and jump freely, just like they did. I longed to be free from the self-absorption that ruled my life. I wanted to live and I wanted to laugh and I wanted to love, but I did not know how.

Chapter 18

The Double Life

I hope you have not been leading a double life, pretending to be wicked and being good all the time. That would be hypocrisy.
OSCAR WILDE, *THE IMPORTANCE OF BEING EARNEST*
He is a double-minded man, unstable in all his ways.
JAMES 1:8 NKJV

It was a hot summer day. My roommates and I lived in a rented house without air conditioning, only adding to the frustration I was already experiencing. I had stopped taking some of my anti-depressant medication, not wanting to rely on prescriptions for the rest of my life. As a result, my emotions were on edge, and I was prone to angry outbursts. The old window in my bedroom wouldn't easily open, and in a fit of rage, I pushed hard on the frame, accidentally forcing the palm of my hand and my wrist through the window pane. Broken glass sliced through my wrist, causing a deep cut. My roommate Mark handed me a clean towel to wrap around my bloody wrist and dropped me off at the emergency room.

I waited alone for what seemed like hours in the ER. When the doctor finally saw me, he said I was lucky that I did not do any permanent nerve damage, since the cut was so deep. The hospital personnel stitched me up and I was on my way, back to a life that was still without any sense of peace. The doctor mended my physical being, but my spiritual sickness was something that no man-made remedy could heal.

I was still desperately looking for total peace and fulfillment, and I was still deceived into thinking Susan could help me find it. My roommates and other friends heard me speak of this mysterious woman, but they never met her. They didn't really know what I was involved with when I would go to AA meetings or to Susan's house. Likewise, Susan didn't know how I spent my day when I wasn't with her. Most of my time was spent alone or with my artsy friends, but Susan's influence was heavy in my life.

Over time, I veered away from the homosexual community, realizing I didn't fit in there either. I saw that the ideology many professed wasn't working for them, and I became frustrated with the whole thing. I was still attracted to women, but I was unwilling to play any more games. I began isolating myself from nearly everyone outside of Susan's group, while still holding to every word that she said.

My involvement with her did much to feed my intellectual pride. Susan was educated and intelligent, and the people I met through her were equally impressive in their knowledge and societal status. One such woman was Maggie, a medical doctor and the daughter of two very prominent physicians who had connections with powerful world leaders. Maggie often traveled with her highly accomplished parents, bringing back photos of herself with well-known people such as Pope John Paul II, Mother Theresa, and others. These were not just casual photos. She actually spent time with many well-known individuals.

On one occasion, Maggie was on her way out of the country to have dinner in a European city. When we asked who she would be having dinner with, we were amazed that former President George H.W. Bush would be there with his family. Maggie was a European-born woman who had come under Susan's counsel after losing her husband to a drug overdose and while dealing with her own alcohol and drug addiction.

Another woman who was part of Susan's network was an ex-fashion model then living in Houston, Texas. She often came to town on business wearing extravagant fur coats and driving a high-dollar convertible. She was a flamboyant and dramatic character with an air of sophistication that was really just a mask to cover up the childish emotionalism that comes with a life of addiction.

I always wanted to be a part of something important. I wanted to be connected with people who were significant in the world's eyes. I prided myself on my connections with those I considered sophisticated and intellectual, even if they were social misfits. And my pride became the amplification for more self-deception.

Hypnosis

On one occasion Susan decided to hypnotize a group of us in her living room. According to her, it was a method that she used in her medical practice as an anesthesiologist. Several of the women there had already experienced hypnosis, but it was a first for me. I didn't believe someone could hypnotize me by counting and saying a few words. But something happened. Once the hypnosis was in effect, I was no longer in control of my being.

Hypnosis is still a controversial subject that scientists and scholars continue to research. However, there are scientific findings that give credence to the fact that there are physiological responses in those under hypnosis.

For me, the session seemed harmless. It was even relaxing and pleasant. Before beginning the session, Susan said that at any point we could ask to be "un-hypnotized" and she would let us out from under the hypnosis. While only a manipulative statement to get us to trust her, it did take away the fear at the time. But this was just another step in Susan taking dominion over my life.

Time went on and I continued to stay sober. One of my friends who had previously been one of Susan's followers warned me to stop listening to Susan, but it was too late. Whatever Susan said, I did. This friend, Cassie, had once been my AA sponsor, and she had my best interests in mind when she called me on the telephone to warn me to get away from Susan. Cassie, too, had once listened to and followed Susan's counsel, but she eventually realized that it was harmful. Unfortunately, I was already too brainwashed to listen to sound advice.

I began to have a number of health problems. Years of living on prescription medications, alcohol, caffeine and nicotine left me malnourished. Add to this the fact that food was never a primary concern during my drinking years, and you've got a recipe for disaster.

Suddenly, I began having extreme back pain—pain to the point that I was unable to work. By this time, I'd finished graduate school and had been sober for more than three years. I was physically alive, but spiritually and emotionally, I might as well have been dead, and my physical health was diminishing quickly. The pain in my back became excruciating, and I quit my job as a grocery store clerk because it required me to stand and to lift.

Due to all of these health difficulties, I decided to return to my hometown, the very place I had always desired to leave. My plan, which seemed a reasonable option at the time, was to live with my parents for a while. Ironically, it was actually Susan's idea that I move back, but that didn't mean that she was out of my life. We still remained connected from a distance.

So I left the city I once loved and returned to the one place I worked so hard to escape. After moving, I kept in touch with Susan via telephone, and she gave me her doctor's orders every time I called her. Once Susan and some other women were taking a trip to Florida, and she insisted I come along, even though I was short on cash. I drove to Lexington to meet them, and we headed south, with Susan as our tyrannical dictator. She was now my full-fledged "doctor," attempting to treat me for the various medical concerns I had. She told me what I could and could not eat, limiting me to barely enough to stay alive. Her instruction caused me to live in fear that almost every type of food would make me sick. Staying away from certain foods became an obsession. All because of the advice of a woman who conveyed her advice about health and nutrition while puffing on a Virginia Slim cigarette.

With suitcases loaded and ready, a small group of us were on our way to sunny Florida in Susan's big boat of a Cadillac for what was to be an enjoyable vacation. But what was supposed to be a nice trip to the beach ended in unexpected horror.

Chapter 19

Following Doctor's Orders

The miserable hath no other medicine but only hope.
WILLIAM SHAKESPEARE, *MEASURE FOR*
MEASURE

If you are cheerful, you feel good; if you are sad, you hurt all
over.

PROVERBS 17:22 CEV

Susan and I sat in her home's dimly lit basement office. She sat across from me in a soft armchair, while I sat in a leather office chair. A long, thin cigarette dangled between her bony fingers. We had just returned from Florida where a number of bizarre conflicts took place between Susan and some of the other women, and Susan was starting to crack. She had always seemed so strong and sophisticated, but she was starting to lose control. Her theories had always been a little extreme, but she now spoke of really odd things, like receiving messages from her deceased brother. She was also growing more and more paranoid—not just about the government, but about some of the people around her. Yet I was still convinced that I needed to listen to her.

We sat together in her office that afternoon, and she decided she wanted to do one more hypnosis session with me. I was desperate for my health to improve and was hoping the hypnosis would offer some healing and relief, so I agreed.

One of her goals during the session was to train my mind to eat a certain way for health reasons. She had more or less controlled what I ate for some time, but the hypnosis process would take it a step further, causing me to fear that I would become sick every time I put food into my mouth. This eventually led to extreme malnourishment.

For several years people accused me of being anorexic. At the time, I couldn't see it, but the reality was that for many years I had eaten less than what my body required. Looking back now, as early as middle school, I felt great pressure to stay thin. There are many mental factors that psychologists attribute to anorexic behavior, the primary one being a drive to stay thin in order to be accepted. I know now that I was subconsciously driven by the fear of being overweight for many years. And on top of the eating disorder that already existed, Susan was instilling in me an even greater fear of food.

The hypnosis session continued. For the rest of the time, her goal was to help me call to memory my own birth. Scientifically, this is a ridiculous notion. But she claimed to be able to do this very thing, although she never mentioned why it was necessary. I believe now that she probably didn't retire from medicine, but was possibly forced out due to her extreme methods of practice.

I'd never been alone with her while under hypnosis. The previous session took place in a group setting, and unlike the first time, this session did not have an atmosphere of relaxation and peace. In fact, I felt very uncomfortable from the beginning but didn't have the courage to back out.

Deep down I knew that contrary to what she had once stated, I did not have the power to ask her to stop. I had already surrendered all of the power to her. Suddenly, a part of me was disgusted by her and the whole situation. But there was no turning back. I had allowed her to have control of every move that I made.

This control was played out while we were in Florida. Susan was speaking to some tourists next to the hotel's swimming pool one afternoon. She referred to me as one of her "patients," and as she talked to them of my health situation, she spoke as though I were one of her experimental subjects on whom she would test her bizarre cures. I had become a laboratory rat in her world of mad science. Throughout the trip, I relegated more and more control to Susan, allowing her to say anything to or about me, without ever defending myself. I simply let her have her way. The hypnosis session was her chance to strike a final blow to my soul.

At one point during the hypnosis, she tried to put words in my mouth. She was supposedly taking me through the memory of my birth and she said that as I was being pulled out of the birth canal my shoulder got caught. She suggested that very uncomfortable pressure was being placed on my shoulder and I was experiencing discomfort because the delivery room was so cold and bright. Then she asked, "Do you remember this?" Of course I didn't remember, because it was all a hoax; but I said, "Yes" because I didn't have the power to disagree.

Around the moment that she suggested the situation with my shoulder, I felt something evil, dreadful, and cold enter into me from the left, just above my shoulder. It was a force that produced the most horrible feeling of being violated, and yet I had nothing with which to resist it. At the time I didn't understand what was happening. I just felt the coldness and the violation of my being.

I didn't understand that a demon had taken up residence in me. I had long since rejected the idea that such spirits even existed, and I would never have imagined such a thing were possible. But it happened; I was possessed with a destructive, taunting, tormenting spirit. This may seem far-fetched to some, but the evidence is in the immediate downward spiral that took place in my mind and body.

The journey I had been traveling for the last several years had led me to reject the existence of one true God. I concluded that the divinity of Jesus was a man-made myth and I rejected the validity of the Bible. Susan and I often discussed the many theories that maintain Jesus was not the Son of God and that he didn't die and resurrect as according to scripture. Susan herself had many theories about how the

Bible came into existence during the Middle Ages and that it was only created to control people.

I myself had a deep hatred for Christians and was not afraid to tell anyone how much I despised their ways. Christians were the brunt of many jokes among my friends and me. In our ignorance of what true Christianity was about, we saw Christians as the enemy, the ones who hindered society from living in freedom. They were the unenlightened ones.

The fact that I'd rejected the idea of God and heaven meant I'd also rejected the idea of Satan, demons, and Hell. So on that August day I had no idea what had just taken place. I only knew that it was extremely uncomfortable. I did not yet realize that I had just lost my mind to a demonic power.

Chapter 20

Out of My Mind

The pain of the mind is worse than the pain of the body.
PUBLILIUS SYRUS
The wicked are too proud to seek God. They seem to think that
God is dead.
PSALM 10:4 NLT

I sat on the back patio of my parents' house reading Francis
Bacon's *Atlantis*. Susan's theories were so instilled in me that I
believed I shared some of her insight. I felt I could read certain
classics and unfold some of the workings of government systems. We
were conspiracy theorists long before the similarly named Mel Gibson
movie made the term a household phrase. Susan had trained me to
study certain aspects of society to determine who was controlling the
government, the universities, and so on. She lived with a huge amount
of paranoia about things to come, and I began to take on the same
paranoia, thinking I had superior knowledge to everyone around me.

On one occasion Susan invited me on a trip to Washington,
D.C., during which she had dinner with an individual who is well
known in some circles for his political writings and affiliations. He

was the protégé of a well-known American writer convicted of treason for his Fascist statements during World War II. Had I gone on the trip, I, too, would have shared dinner with this writer. Again, my pride was inflated because of my associations with those I considered insightful.

As I sat on the patio that day, I no longer delighted in our previous discussions and intellectual exercises. Rather, I saw them as burdens. I desired none of the knowledge I'd sold my soul to own. I felt alone, that there was no one with whom I could associate.

I began attending AA meetings in a new town, but they were different than what I was used to. My hometown was much smaller than Lexington, and most of the AA people seemed extremely dysfunctional and less sophisticated than their big city counterparts. But I believed I needed the meetings, so I attended regularly. It was strange to be in meetings with people from my hometown—people I knew by name.

In the weeks following the Florida trip with Susan, my health began to decline quickly. I was very weak and exhausted all of the time. Susan was still my "doctor," and she would prescribe bizarre remedies over the phone. She still insisted that I remain on a very strict diet.

But something profoundly powerful and evil had happened in our previous meeting, and the results became quickly evident. In a very short time, a variety of strange symptoms emerged. My mind became hazy and unclear. Eventually, I lost much of my short-term memory. I became very sickly and had excruciating back pain, and I became very jaundiced. My hair, which had always been healthy, became extremely oily and unmanageable. No matter how often I washed it, my hair was dirty and unkempt. My entire body was changing.

Because my mind was in such a fog, I can't recall when the physical changes took place, but I soon felt sick and nauseous to the point that I could barely get out of bed. Most of the time, unless I was attending an AA meeting or working a few hours from home as a telemarketer, I would lie on my stomach with my arms down by my side. It was difficult to move from this position, and the physical pain continued to intensify.

Another situation arose that was quite ironic. My involvement with Susan had, in my mind, brought maturity to my thinking and intellect. However, I noticed that my emotional level was regressing and I started to think like a small child. While my intellect stayed at the same level, my emotional state was that of a little girl who was extremely needy and insecure.

I became totally hopeless and helpless, wishing to go back to the days of being drunk and suicidal, because those days seemed like a cakewalk compared to what I was now going through. I would have easily traded the pain of psychiatric hospitals and rehabilitation centers for the mental torment I suffered.

I wished I could trade my life for anyone else's on the planet. I had never felt that way before, even during my lowest times. I had always wanted to be me—even when I considered suicide. But now that had all changed. I didn't even know who I was any more.

When I took a telephone call from a family member in an emergency situation, I should have passed information to another person, but failed to do so because I was in a haze and completely forgot about the telephone call.

Next came trouble with my eyes. I'd always had nearly perfect eyesight, but I began to have difficulty seeing. I didn't need glasses. Rather, it was taking great energy and concentration to focus. If I did not make a concerted effort to see, everything would go blurry and my mind would drift off as if daydreaming.

Then I had trouble with my hearing. It was as if my ears would clog up, causing me to experience hearing loss. It seemed all of my senses were failing me. However, one of the most troubling difficulties was when it became difficult to talk.

It wasn't like I had laryngitis. It was not at all like a person having a cold and sore throat and losing his or her voice. Rather, it became extremely difficult for me to project my voice. I had no strength to project sound and to let myself be heard. I always had a fairly strong voice, but now the strength of my vocal chords was fading. I was extremely weak in every sense of the word.

At the same time, I was becoming stiff, immobile, and almost lifeless. It was difficult to move, and I was in constant pain, particularly in my back. At one point, I couldn't remember the last time I laughed. It had been months.

I spent what little energy I had trying to get better. I was still holding on to much of the teaching I gathered while living in Lexington, such as Scientology and New Age concepts. As I laid in pain day after day, I began to expand my horizons and read books by Edgar Cayce, who was known for his alleged psychic abilities. There were no limits to my exploration.

Other efforts to get well included spending exorbitant amounts of money on herbal remedies, based on the recommendations of a mostly toothless man operating out of the back room of a health food store; visiting a Catholic nun who performed healing touch for a fee; and participating in a practice in which sick people call on dead loved ones to relieve pain and disease. These were just some of my frantic efforts to receive a miracle in my life.

The Bible talks about a woman who also made desperate attempts to get well. (Luke 8, Mark 5). Mark 5:25–26 says, "A woman in the crowd had suffered for twelve years with constant bleeding. She had suffered a great deal from many doctors, and over the years she had spent everything she had to pay them, but she had gotten no better. In fact, she had gotten worse." (NLT) I likewise grew worse with each attempt to get well, spending every penny I had. I began to accept that death was inevitable.

Many days I believed I would lie down and not get back up. Because I had been immersed in New Age thinking, I believed my spirit would just float off into space somewhere. I actually wanted to die so that I might finally find some peace and relief. In the meantime,

I continued to use mind over matter in an attempt to somehow achieve healing and peace, but they never came.

I was financially broke, had no health insurance, and did not believe that the traditional medical establishment could help me. However, a doctor whose practice was a couple of hours away had a reputation for being open to alternative remedies, so I made an appointment to see him. When I arrived at his office, he took one look at me and knew I was seriously sick. My skin was yellow and I was thin and frail. I looked like death. He ran several tests but wanted to run more than I could afford. He said his prediction was that I had some form of cancer or a rare, incurable virus. Discouraged and broke, I went home to die.

Chapter 21

The Prison of My Mind

Stone walls do not a prison make, nor iron bars a cage.
RICHARD LOVELACE, *TO ALTHEA FROM PRISON*
Set me free from my prison, that I may praise your name.
PSALM 142:7 NKJV

I sat in Aunt Shirley's living room. I stopped by her home for a short visit, knowing that Aunt June was staying there. These two aunts were my dad's sisters. Aunt June had always been interested in natural remedies and government conspiracies, so we had some common ground. She sat in a chair across from me. I was still weak and in a lot of pain. We chatted a little bit about my health, but I will never forget her words as she looked me straight in the eyes.

"Amy, I am concerned for your health," Aunt June said, "but I am more concerned about your soul." Her words shot through me like lightning. I was stunned. If anyone had spoken to me in the past about the condition of my soul, I would have written that person off as a religious fanatic. Yet out of shear desperation, I was willing to listen. Something told me that I needed to embrace every word she had to say.

I always knew that Aunt June was different than most of my relatives. She had a habit of handing out boxes and boxes of paperback copies of the New Testament, written in an easy-to-understand translation. As a child, I received one of the New Testament paperbacks from her. My Catholic upbringing never emphasized Bible reading, so it was unusual to be encouraged to read the Bible for my own enrichment. I don't know what the other members of my family did with their copies, but I read mine as a young girl and was intrigued with the words and actions of Jesus I found on those pages.

There was always an unspoken agreement to disregard what Aunt June had to say. Suddenly, that changed. I was willing to listen, not just with my head, but also with my heart.

At this point in life, I had begun working in a prison. My health was still disastrous, but with the persuasion of my family, I attained a job as a prison librarian. Not exactly my lifelong ambition, but it was a professional position in which I was the director of a library, even if it was for prisoners. In addition to overseeing the functions of an informational library, I had the responsibility of overseeing a full law library, an inmate newspaper, and about twenty inmate workers. I did all of this while still having major health and physical issues. There were times when I was so weak I walked alongside the wall to hold myself up.

Working in the midst of convicted murderers, rapists, and thieves was no easy job, particularly for someone with so many issues. I was forced to endure the inmates' attempts to manipulate and intimidate me in this position that was officially categorized as "hazardous duty."

All I saw each day at prison symbolized my own life. The huge fences topped with layers of barbed wire were a metaphor for the prison of my own mind. I was trapped in a mind that wasn't my own. I had no idea who I was. Each morning, I went through several security checkpoints, occasionally being searched for items that were forbidden in the prison. I hated the feeling of being violated in that way. It was a symbol of my own spirit being violated because I had never had any weapons powerful enough to guard it. The searches made by the prison officers also reminded me that I had much to hide. My life was riddled with the fear that something would be exposed that had been hidden long ago. I carried so much shame because of the life I had lived. I had been a liar, a cheater, a thief, a slanderer, a lawbreaker, and a woman who had descended to degradingly low moral standards.

Walking past the solitary confinement unit of the prison day after day reminded me of just how alone I was. Seeing the inmates who were serving life sentences reminded me that I, too, was wasting my dreams and visions, and that I was not free to be happy in my world.

The prison was surrounded by a wooded area on one side, and a marshy area on the other. The entire landscape was often steeped in thick fog, particularly in the morning. I'm sure there were sunny days there, but I only recall the gray, wet, dismal days that matched my existence.

Driving the forty-five minute route to the prison was arduous, and I had to push myself to make it each day. Perhaps in all of the darkness, there was still some glimmer of hope, some drive to survive.

It was during this time that my odd medical issues began to surface. My voice became weak, and I began to lose my hearing. While visiting another prison library in the state, my hearing left completely. I watched the librarian's lips move but couldn't hear what she was saying, so I nodded as though I could understand her.

My symptoms persisted even as I forced myself to go to work every day. I am still amazed that I was able to keep going with the pain, weakness, and nausea. There must have been someone praying for me in my darkest hour.

The Bible speaks of a man who was brought to Jesus for healing. Matthew 12:22 says, "Then a demon-possessed man, who was **blind and couldn't speak**, was brought to Jesus. He healed the man so that he could both speak and see." (NLT) Two of the symptoms I experienced after receiving a tormenting spirit were diminishing sight and diminishing power in my voice. According to scripture, these two symptoms can go hand in hand with demon possession.

In another place in scripture, there is the story of a boy who was tormented by an evil spirit. Mark 9:17–18 says, *"One of the men* in the crowd spoke up and said, 'Teacher, I brought my son so you could heal him. He is possessed by **an evil spirit that won't let him talk**. And whenever this spirit seizes him, it throws him violently to the ground. Then he foams at the mouth and grinds his teeth and becomes **rigid**.'" (NLT) Here we see two more symptoms associated with an evil spirit, symptoms that I experienced to a degree. The boy was mute, his body rigid. When I began to lose the ability to project my voice, my body became stiff and rigid.

We also read that the boy mentioned in Mark, chapter 9, had hearing loss. In verse 25, Jesus says, "You **deaf** and **mute** spirit, I command you, come out of him and never enter him again." I likewise experienced diminished hearing after being possessed with a demonic spirit.

I never did become fully blind, deaf, immobile, or mute, but perhaps if the tormenting spirit continued to have its way in me, that would have been my doom. It was within a couple of weeks after the final hypnosis session with Susan that these symptoms began to take over my body and torment took over my mind.

The Bible makes it clear that there are varying degrees of power among demons. Matthew 12:45 says, "Then the spirit finds seven other spirits **more evil than itself**, and they all enter the person and live there. And so that person is worse off than before. That will be the experience of this evil generation." (NLT) So we know that demon possession affects its victims to varying degrees. The degree to which I was affected may not have driven me to some of the extreme

93

behaviors that have been recorded concerning other demon-possessed people. However, the level of mental torment I experienced was indescribably extreme.

As I sat with Aunt June and listened to the possibility that there may be an answer to all of my pain, I began the process of opening my heart to a loving Savior who desired to set me free even more than I desperately desired it. I listened to Aunt June explain how to call on the name of the Lord and be saved. My heart began to open up as I listened to her particular testimony of divine healing.

She shared the story of what took place in her life 30 years prior. Like all my extended family, Aunt June was brought up in the Catholic Church and attended mass regularly. But unlike many of her Catholic counterparts, she read the Bible often and believed everything it said. She took literally what she read and placed it deep in her heart until her faith for miracles was built.

When her children were young, she began to have a problem with her foot and was unable to walk on it. At that time, she lived in Louisville, Kentucky, and attended a church there. Thirty years earlier, she stood up in that Catholic Church and stated that she believed that if the elders of the church prayed for her, she would be healed of the infirmity in her foot. She quoted James 5:14–15. "Is anyone among you sick? Let them call the elders of the church to pray over them and anoint them with oil in the name of the Lord. And the prayer offered in faith will make the sick person well; the Lord will raise them up. If they have sinned, they will be forgiven." In response

94

to this verse, the priest and some others agreed to lay hands on her and pray for her.

As they prayed, Aunt June felt heat course through her body, as though a hot poker went from the top of her head, through her body, and out of her non-working foot. She was instantly healed and never had any more problems walking. It was an amazing story and I knew she was telling the truth. Something inside of me desperately wanted to believe that there was also a miracle for me and my desperate situation.

This thinking conflicted with everything I had convinced myself of for a number of years. That Jesus could actually be the Son of God challenged my previous conceptions. From my Aunt June I was hearing about an aspect of Jesus I'd never heard before. Was it possible that He was more than just a carved figure on a cross, like I had seen in church all my life? Was it possible that He was alive and well, and still relevant to people today? Was it possible that He could save me from my sickness and misery? Was it possible that good and evil existed, and that a sovereign God existed? Was it possible that I really needed a Savior to redeem me from my sin?

I went home and pondered these questions. I even tried to pray, crying out to God in the best way I knew. My mouth hung open for about two weeks in total shock from the news I had just received, as I pondered the possibility that this Jesus, whom I had boldly proclaimed was just a mythical figure, was actually real and was actually the Son of God.

Chapter 22

A Daring Visit

Courage is the ladder on which all the other virtues mount.

CLARE BOOTH LUCE

And don't be afraid of the people, for I will be with you and will protect you. I, the LORD, have spoken!

JOSHUA 1:8 NLT

I was in the upstairs office of a co-worker's house when I picked up the telephone and made a very daring call. Aunt June suggested I find a church affiliated with her denomination. For some time, she had been attending a Full Gospel church that believed divine healing is provided through the wounds (or stripes) of Jesus. Her knowledge of God's healing power was based on Isaiah 53:5, in which the Old Testament prophet declared that both spiritual and physical healing would be made available to those who receive Jesus as their Lord and Savior. "But he was pierced for our transgressions, he was crushed for our iniquities; the punishment that brought us peace was upon him, and by his wounds we are healed." (NIV)

This idea is reiterated in the New Testament in 1 Peter 2:24, which says, "He personally carried our sins in his body on the cross so that we can be dead to sin and live for what is right. By his wounds **you are healed**." (NLT) This was the very idea that captured my attention. Healing was what I was desperate for, so I decided to locate a church near the prison facility where I was employed. I flipped through the phone book, called a local church, and spoke with the pastor. I made plans to attend the morning worship service the following Sunday.

When I arrived at the small red brick church building, I had no idea what to expect, but I was ready for anything that would move me from agony to peace. I was willing to do just about anything asked of me. Nothing would stop me now that I had glimpsed the possibility of a real encounter with my Creator.

I still didn't have much understanding about a real relationship with a loving God, but I'd tried most everything else to appease my empty soul, so off to church I went.

The church was in a town of only about 3,000 people and the congregation met in a small, older building. There were very few in the gathering that first morning I attended. After I arrived and took a seat near the back, the music started, and everyone stood. The song lyrics were projected on a drop-down screen using an old light-operated projector, and I was amazed when the first song ended and the music team started to sing another. This was so different than the

Catholic churches of my upbringing, where we sang only one opening hymn before moving to the introduction of mass.

I was really shocked when we began to sing a third song. I was almost embarrassed about the whole situation. This backwoods church, with its continual singing, was rather strange. It seemed a little redundant. I was ready to get on with God's miracle-working power, though I had no idea what this should look like. My soul longed for change, but I still didn't understand what a relationship with God was all about. And still the music continued.

The worship music team was led by a piano player, who was also the singer and the pastor's wife. Only one other musician accompanied her. He was a young man on acoustic guitar. When the music ended, the pastor preached an energetic and passionate sermon that I don't recall a word of. I only remember being very uncomfortable as He proclaimed the Word of God. The tormenting spirit inside of me wanted to rise up and tell the minister to shut up, and I struggled to contain the urge to scream out. There was a battle taking place in my mind, and part of me began to doubt that this was the place for me. I thought that maybe it was just another in my series of passing phases. Yet, something in my inmost being told me to stick it out.

The uncomfortable, uneventful service ended, and several people introduced themselves to me. One was Alice. She was very bold in her faith, and she began speaking to me about the kingdom of God and the power of the gospel. I knew almost immediately that she'd had some sort of experience in her life that was very real to her. I wanted her to tell me more.

I also met the guitar player and was interested in getting to know him. A bass guitar player myself, I was naturally drawn to other musicians. I eventually got to spend time with this very special guitarist, and I know him very well today, since he is now my husband! But our marriage was still a long way off. I only said hello to him that day.

I went back for several Sundays and was always ready to speak with Alice. She began to give me all kinds of literature on divine healing, the baptism of the Holy Spirit, and the power of faith, which were all things I knew very little about. I was hungry to absorb all she had to say. I appreciated her willingness to share her faith and knowledge of God with me.

The pastor and his wife became a little concerned that Alice was bombarding me with too much information too fast. They were a very sweet young couple trying to keep the doors of the small church open. Their concern for my spiritual well-being was genuine, and they didn't want me overwhelmed by too much knowledge too fast. But I couldn't get enough. I was still desperate for relief in my body, mind, and spirit.

Alice invited me to a women's Bible study held in the courthouse building of the city. I don't recall what she told me to expect, but there must have been some indication that I would see the power of God in action. I was extremely hungry to experience a real encounter with God like Aunt June had told me about. Finally, I had a glimmer of hope.

Chapter 23

Power From Above

O Holy Spirit, descend plentifully into my heart. Enlighten the dark corners of this neglected dwelling and scatter there Thy cheerful beams.

SAINT AUGUSTINE

And He said to her, "Daughter, your faith has made you well. Go in peace, and be healed of your affliction."

JESUS IN MARK 8:34 NKJV

It was a warm spring evening as I climbed the stairs to the Central City, Kentucky courthouse. I'd been working at the prison for about six months, and while I was still extremely sick in my body and still imprisoned in a mind ruled by darkness, I held on to a glimmer of hope that I might find a way out of my desperate situation. In fact, I was determined to find freedom no matter the price.

The miraculous encounter I hungered for eluded me, but I wasn't going to stop looking. That is why I was willing to attend a meeting in a courthouse with total strangers. Alice, who invited me, didn't even show up until the meeting was nearly over. But what took place between the time I arrived and the time Alice appeared is the very event that has changed my life forever!

All of the women in attendance sat on metal chairs arranged in a circle. The leader announced that we would be hearing from a guest speaker later in the evening. But first, we were going to spend some time worshiping God. I knew very little about worship at that point, but I stood up with the other women. There was no music, but the women began to sing a song most of them knew. As they sang with eyes closed and hands lifted, no one paid attention to anyone else in the room. They were all absorbed in the moment, with their attention on the One they adored. I remember thinking that since no one was watching me, I might try lifting my hands as well. I had never participated in such a practice, but why not try?

As the singing continued, I heard an amazing sound—the most beautiful and amazing sound I'd ever heard. There were only about fifteen women in the room, but they sounded like a massive choir singing in one of the best acoustically designed buildings in the world. It was spectacular, and I knew that small group of women couldn't create a sound like that on their own. It could only have been a heavenly host of angels!

Then there was another unusual manifestation I had recently heard about but not experienced. Some of the women started to sing in an unknown language. I know now that it was a heavenly language, as is seen in the New Testament of the Bible, particularly Acts. It was unlike anything I had ever heard. Although this was all very new to me, nothing in me questioned the validity of what was happening. I knew it was God!

As the singing progressed, a young woman started jumping up and down, exclaiming, "I'm free! I'm free!" She was not at all hindered or self-conscious. She was obviously having a marvelous time. I somehow knew that what she was declaring was the result of God's healing power transforming her life. I never found out her story, but someone that radical and exuberant about God had experienced a great transformation in her own life. As she jumped and shouted, she appeared almost foolish and childish, yet something inside of me yearned for that kind of freedom and boldness.

Then I experienced my "suddenly." As if out of nowhere, a sensation like electricity shot through my extended fingertips and began to pulsate down my arms and then into my whole body. I knew immediately that it was God Himself. I was engulfed in Holy Spirit power and fire. It was like nothing I'd ever imagined possible. A very real and tangible force was surging through me, seeming to affect every cell in my body. But the sensation was most evident in my hands and arms. The experience was intense—so intense that it could have been frightening, but I was not scared at all. In fact, the feeling was so good I didn't want it to end. I opened my eyes and began to watch my hands contort as I held them in the air in front of me.

There were two forces at work: one trying to free me, the other refusing to leave my body. I still had full control of my body's movement, yet something was pulling my fingers and hands inward. My hands curled up unless I forcefully opened them back up again. It was like a live science-fiction movie. The God of the universe had stepped in to reclaim me as one of His. The tormenting spirit was being put on notice, and the One who came to set me free was going to win!

Several of the women understood that the Lord was touching me in a powerful way. They came and stood next to me, put their hands on my shoulders and my back, and prayed. The sensation of electricity continued until a climactic impulse of power surged through my body and threw me backwards through the air, until I landed peacefully in a chair. It seemed as if the woman in front of me had punched me into mid-air, but she was much too small to have applied the immensity of force that threw me backward.

When I landed in the chair, total peace came over me. In an instant, I was saved, healed, and delivered. I opened my heart to Jesus, welcoming Him in as my Savior and Lord, and I knew I would never be the same.

The tormenting spirit was gone, as were the pain in my body and the confusion of my mind. There was an instantaneous change in my physical make-up. The excruciating pain in my back was gone, my mind was suddenly clear, and my short-term memory was reinstated. I could think with clarity once again, as total peace and love flooded my being.

At the time, I was untrained in the supernatural realm and the power of God's kingdom, so I wasn't fully aware of all that had happened. But I knew it was all the work of Jesus. I told one of the women who prayed with me that I believed that I had been dramatically healed. She acknowledged that when she was praying with me, she felt something leave my body. I'm not sure anyone there understood that a resident tormenting spirit had been cast out of me. All that mattered at the moment was that I had been set free by the power of God.

Chapter 24

Power in His Presence

I want the presence of God Himself, or I don't want anything at all to do with religion... I want all that God has or I don't want any.

A.W. TOZER

Come out of the man, unclean spirit.

JESUS IN MARK 5:8 NKJV

A demon spirit was cast out of me. At one time this would have seemed like something from a fairy tale or an ancient myth. My scientific and intellectual mind would have dismissed such an idea as a ridiculous and uneducated assessment of the world in which we live. But in this case, experiential knowledge outweighed my previous philosophical knowledge.

However, I was still puzzled and had a series of questions. The main one was this: If my mind had been ruled by a demon, how had I been provoked to participate in worshiping God during a women's Bible study? How was it that I was willing to lift my hands to Him, in adoration of who He is? It didn't make sense.

Thankfully, God, through the Holy Spirit, brought understanding to me through the gospel of Mark, in which the power of the Holy Spirit is seen over and over. Often called the "Revelator," the Holy Spirit brings revelation to us as individuals in God's kingdom. While Jesus was on the earth, He said He must go away so that the Holy Spirit can come. One of the great mysteries is that there is only one God who He exists in three persons: the Father, Son, and Holy Spirit.

Jesus is now seated next to God the Father in Heaven, while the Holy Spirit is on Earth, with the ability to be everywhere at once! The Holy Spirit became a guide for me during my new way of life, and God began to answer my questions. As believers in Christ, we have twenty-four hour access to the Holy Spirit. And this is what the Lord showed me.

I had an experience similar to the demon-possessed man in the book of Mark, chapter 5. Although he was possessed with multiple demons and was well beyond sanity, when Jesus stepped onto the shore, the demon-possessed man ran to Jesus and worshiped Him.

> Then they came to the other side of the sea, to the
> country of the Gadarenes. And when He had come out
> of the boat, immediately there met Him out of the
> tombs a man with an unclean spirit, who had his
> dwelling among the tombs; and no one could bind him,
> not even with chains, because he had often been bound
> with shackles and chains. And the chains had been
> pulled apart by him, and the shackles broken in pieces;

neither could anyone tame him. And always, night and day, he was in the mountains and in the tombs, crying out and cutting himself with stones.

When he saw Jesus from afar, **he ran and worshiped Him.** (Mark 5:1-6, NKJV)

I finally had my answer. When Jesus came near, the man couldn't help himself. He had to worship Him. And the same was true for me. Verse 6 says that the demon-possessed man "ran and worshiped" Jesus. Think about that. One who was ruled by Satan's cohorts became a worshiper. Jesus was his answer, and when he ran to Jesus, the man found peace and relief. I, too, stepped into Jesus' presence, and in His presence worship became an automatic response. His response to our worship is always more of His love. His love drew me, and that same love freed me.

This passage from the book of Mark is a clear demonstration of the power of Jesus. He is not simply a loving and gentle Savior, although that certainly is a part of His personality. He is also a mighty Healer, Deliverer, and Redeemer! Every power in the universe has to bow to His power. When Jesus confronted the demons who held this man captive for so long, they had to submit to Him.

And when Jesus confronted the tormenting spirit in me, it also had to bow to His power. I became a new person in an instant, and nothing would ever be the same!

Chapter 25

Even the Grass Is Greener

Don't ask yourself what the world needs. Ask yourself what
makes you come alive and then go do that. Because what the
world needs is people who have come alive.

HOWARD THURMAN

Go to the Temple and give the people this message of life!

ACTS 5:20 NLT

Life was immediately new. Even the long drive to the prison
took on a different appearance. The winding western Kentucky roads
were no longer oppressive and dreary, and the grassy farms I drove
past were suddenly transformed into bright and colorful displays of
God's glory.

I was a new creation on the inside. 2 Corinthians 5:17 says, "If
anyone is in Christ, he is a new creation. Old things pass away, and all
things are made new." That was one of the first scriptures I learned
and one of the first I saw working in my life. Jesus lived inside me,
and He made my spirit new through the power of the Holy Spirit.

I became extremely hungry for God's Word. Every word I
read from the Bible was alive, and the words leapt off the page as if
each word were written just for me. What had once seemed a boring,

ancient, irrelevant book now contained the most important words I could put into my being. John 3:16, which I looked up years earlier after seeing it on a sign held high in the stands of an NFL game, finally made sense: "For God so loved the world that He gave His only begotten Son, that whoever believes in Him might not perish but have everlasting life." (NIV) I have entered into that everlasting life, having been snatched from death, and I am going to live with Him forever. All because of His love and the power of the selfless act of Jesus who died on a painful cross for me. It is not through any act I have performed or through anything I have earned.

The next verse, John 3:17, is just as meaningful to me. "For God did not send His Son into the world to condemn the world but that the world through Him might be saved." (NIV) How amazing that I am no longer condemned, despite the evil that once motivated me. The God of the Universe has declared me innocent because of the precious blood of His Son. Our guilt and shame are never too much for God! He is merciful! Psalm 86:5 says, "For You, Lord, are good and ready to forgive, and abundant in mercy to all those who call upon You." (NKJV)

It is not by my good works that I have been saved. It is not through religion. It is by the faith that emerged as Jesus' Spirit drew me to Him, and it is through true repentance of my sin. Romans 10:9–10 says, "If you confess with your mouth, 'Jesus is Lord,' and believe in your heart that God raised him from the dead, you will be saved.

For it is with your heart that you believe and are justified, and it is with your mouth that you confess and are saved." (NIV)

2 Corinthians 7:10 says, "Godly sorrow brings repentance that leads to salvation and leaves no regret, but worldly sorrow brings death." (NIV) I was truly sorry for every act in my life that was offensive to God. In His mercy, God revealed all of my sin to me. What I once considered acceptable behavior I could no longer justify. God revealed a new standard to me. It was that simple—I was truly sorry for all that I had done, and I accepted that God was willing to wash away my sin so I could have a true relationship with Him.

Chapter 26

He Loves Us

He loves like a hurricane / I am a tree / Bending beneath the weight of his wind and mercy.

JOHN MARK MCMILLAN

There is no greater love than to lay down one's life for one's friends.

JESUS IN JOHN 15:13 NLT

Writing my story has been a process. I wasn't sure how my past would be welcomed by other believers. Likewise, I wasn't sure how those who oppose Christianity would feel about me sharing my experience with a man named Jesus. But I believe that He wanted me to tell my story. The good news is that Jesus has always loved me, just the way I am. He loved me just as much when I was celebrating sin as He does now. His love is nothing we can earn. It is truly unconditional. He loves because that is who He is—period.

I first began understanding His love when I experienced it from other people who knew me intimately—believers who took me under their wings and taught me. That is why God wants his people in community, spending time with one another. It is during those times

112

that we draw strength and encouragement as we walk through this journey together. Those are the occasions we learn that we can be accepted despite our faults and failures.

In my early days as a believer, I was blessed to experience a church that was alive and full of the spirit of God. In that atmosphere, loved flowed freely. The people were full of faith, full of praise and worship, and full of hunger for God's presence. It was there that I began to sense just how much God loved me.

I know that not everyone attending church and searching for God has had the same experience. Some churches are dead and dry. Some are cold and unloving, and need to awaken to who God really is. People are human, and oftentimes we are poor representatives of the God who lovingly created us. If you have had negative experiences with churches, you have experienced religion. You've been in the midst of people we are warned about in 2 Timothy 3:5: "They will act religious, but they will reject the power that could make them godly." (NLT) These people go through the motions of serving God, but don't do it with the heart. Their love has grown cold.

But God's love never, ever grows cold. Oftentimes, I sense the Lord speaking to my spirit and telling me how much He loves me, which he tells me over and over. If you've never sensed God telling you of His great love for you, why not ask Him about it? Go ahead, I dare you!

A relationship with Him is in direct opposition to following a list of rules. Freedom in Him means freedom from religious ritual. I have a dear friend who often says this of religion, "I'm just not good at it." Guess what? Neither am I. But every day, I am getting better at receiving His grace, which empowers us to walk as He walked.

Through His abundant power and grace, I am a new creation. I no longer rely on alcohol for my peace. Psychiatric medications and recreational drugs are no longer a part of my life. Through the supernatural power of God, I have been sober and in my right mind for many years now.

God doesn't do anything halfway. He has blessed me with a loving husband and two wonderful sons. He has given me the life He always wanted me to have.

Part II

Called to Freedom

Chapter 1

Free From Religion

The LORD doesn't see things the way you see them. People judge by outward appearance, but the LORD looks at the heart.

1 SAMUEL 16:7 NLT

After more than ten years, my husband still teases me about the purple "Little House on the Prairie" dress I purchased at Goodwill shortly after becoming a believer. I wore the dress when I was baptized in water several months after my journey with Jesus began. Believing that dressing like the other people at our little country church would make me more spiritual, I traded my t-shirts and contemporary clothing for skirts and dresses I wouldn't have been caught dead in before. My intentions were good. My theology was not.

When God tells His New Covenant people to be separated from the world, He's not speaking of fashion or keeping man-made traditions (and believe me, there are many man-made traditions in the modern church). The New Testament continually emphasizes an inner transformation that will manifest itself outwardly through our character and behavior, not our ability to follow modern-day church culture and tradition.

1 John 2 commands us not to love the world or the things in the world. The scripture goes on to say that the reason for this is that the world is ruled by lust and pride, elements of the world that we are to steer clear of. This doesn't mean that we avoid the world altogether and become cloistered groups who make no impact on the culture. Quite the contrary. Jesus commanded his disciples to "go into all the world, making disciples." (Matthew 28:19, NKJV)

Note: The church of which I was a part never told me how to dress. In fact, they opened their doors to people from all walks of life. But because many of the regular people dressed a certain way, I immaturely followed suit. (No pun intended). My heart was pure and genuine, and I was willing to sacrifice anything for a loving Savior who set me free from years of torment. I was willing to do anything to see Him face to face and experience more of Him. While I was willing to lay down my life so that others could come into His wonderful kingdom, how I dressed wasn't a prerequisite for any of this. An obedient heart was all He desired.

My purple dress, purchased for a few bucks at a thrift store due to my lack of finances at the time, is a statement about the way certain expectations are imposed on believers. In some churches, there are negative vibes when someone is culturally different from the rest of the congregation. My favorite answer to this conundrum is that God never makes two snowflakes alike. No two trees on the entire planet have branches that flow precisely like the branches of any other tree. God loves diversity!

I became aware of the lack of diversity in my denomination when I visited the state-wide camp meetings. These were large gatherings of believers from all over the state, and the meetings were often refreshing and powerful times with Jesus. The experiences helped me grow in God, thanks to some very good teaching.

But everyone looked like clones of one another. One year, a popular fashion for men was a solid-color shirt with a matching silk tie. At the camp meeting, a huge majority of men sported the same look, but with various color choices. The hairstyles were all nearly identical as well. And wouldn't you know it: most of the attending pastors drove similar "preacher rides," which were usually Cadillacs.

How does this look and feel to an outsider? The underlying message is, "Look like us if you want to be part of us." It created confusion and exclusion, whether intentional or not. I wanted to walk with the Lord and grow in my spiritual life, and this was the particular place I found to do it. So for a little while, I continued with the bad fashions. And let me make myself very clear. The issue here is not clothing. The issue is freedom. The Bible says, "Therefore if the Son makes you free, you shall be free indeed." (John 8:36, NKJV) Aside from provocative and degrading clothing, I don't think God cares if I wear a fancy dress, torn jeans, or a burlap sack. He just wants me to love and obey Him with all my heart.

There is a wonderful scriptural gem in Romans 14, which says, "Blessed is the man who does not condemn himself in that which he approves." (Romans 14:22, NIV) In other words, if we're not commanded to do or not do something, there is freedom. If God's word is specific about something being required, we must obey His words; likewise, if we are commanded not to do something, but do it anyway, it is sin, and we should repent and receive forgiveness. But God says this in Galatians 5:1: "Now make sure that you stay free, and don't get tied up again in slavery to the law." (NLT) Part of the liberty being addressed here involves freedom from religious and man-made rules and regulations.

One of the reasons I use this particular issue of dress code is that pressure to conform had been a huge issue all of my life. It's part of what drove me toward alcohol as a coping mechanism. Feeling I was never free to be myself caused so much loneliness and despair, but Jesus came to "to set the oppressed free." (Luke 4:18, NLT)

There are many things that God will, in His time, change in our lives. He gives us the freedom to follow His word and His presence, and to wait for His instructions for change in our inward hearts and outward actions. My prayer is that many new believers will come into the kingdom of God and find true freedom and diversity there. When we understand this, we will have true unity.

Although it took several years, I no longer have issues with clothing and church. The Bible is clear that the church consists of believers and followers of our Lord Jesus Christ. Church is not a building or a meeting. Buildings are simply gathering places for believers. Being the church is a 24/7 commitment. It means serving God and ministering to people no matter where I go or what I'm wearing. Aren't you thankful that God does not see as man sees? Man looks at the outward appearance, but God looks at the heart.

Chapter 2

Free From Oppression

And you know that God anointed Jesus of Nazareth with the Holy Spirit and with power. Then Jesus went around doing good and healing all who were oppressed by the devil, for God was with him.

ACTS 10:38 NLT

When I was about five years old, my parents allowed me to go on a daring journey – all the way to the drug store about two blocks away from our house. A girl named Cathy from next door invited my sister and me to go with her. We were very excited about venturing on foot to the other end of our dead-end street, which met up with the back parking lot of a small shopping center. Our parents gave my sister and me each a nickel to buy some gum or candy. We were to return home immediately after making our purchase.

When we arrived at the small strip mall, we didn't go to the drug store as planned. At Cathy's request, we went to King's department store a few doors down. Cathy wanted to do some more elaborate shopping, so we ended up on a detour. After browsing for a while, she found a little yellow sun dress, went to the dressing room to try it on, and decided to purchase the dress after some debating about whether or not she should. As we approached the checkout lane, Cathy spotted an Elvis coffee mug on clearance. She decided she must have that as well. All of this took much more time than our simple trip should have. The cashier totaled Cathy's merchandise, and Cathy was a few cents short. I offered my nickel to help.

As we left the store, an older boy from the neighborhood was walking toward us and vehemently stated that half the neighborhood had been out looking for us. Our parents were worried that we were lost. I immediately panicked, afraid of how much trouble I might be in with Mom and Dad. I felt really bad about the whole ordeal. Not only did I have to walk home with the fear of being reprimanded, but I also didn't get any gum or candy because my nickel was gone.

My parents were forgiving and weren't overly angry with us. They had simply been worried. But looking back, I see the beginning of a pattern in my behavior. Instead of speaking up for myself and emphasizing that the purpose of our little journey was to go to the drug store, I let someone else dictate what I would do. And instead of seeing myself as a girl worthy of a five cent piece of bubble gum, I turned my small change over to someone else, not out of generosity, but out of a feeling of little self-worth.

I subconsciously thought that others deserved good things, while I deserved nothing. I thought others should be able to lord themselves over me, while I became a figure in the background, always allowing other kids to pass me up in childhood activities. Had I done this out of a generous heart to see others blessed, it would have

123

been okay. But my motives were based on an incorrect understanding of who God created me to be. I saw everyone else as the "head" while I saw myself as the "tail." As I allowed others to rule over me, I was setting a lifelong pattern that would open the door for Satan to rule over me.

Acts 10:38 tells us that part of Jesus' mission was to heal those who were oppressed by the devil. The original Greek word for oppressed is a word that means "to exercise dominion against." In other words, Jesus wants us to be free from having Satan lord his power over us.

When God placed Adam and Eve in the Garden of Eden, he made them in His image. Genesis 1:27 says, "So God created man in His own image; in the image of God He created him; male and female He created them." (NKJV) The fact that God created a living creature to reflect Himself is a profound concept. His desire is that we be like Him, with all of His traits.

Next He gave the first man and woman authority over all the earth. "Then God blessed them, and God said to them, 'Be fruitful and multiply; fill the earth and subdue it; have dominion over the fish of the sea, over the birds of the air, and over every living thing that moves on the earth.'" (Genesis 1:28, NKJV)

As part of God's creation, the human race was given the responsibility of ruling over the earth. Although the earth belongs to the Lord (Psalm 24), He created man to have authority over all creation. Through Jesus, we have the power to defeat the oppression brought about by Satan. In Luke 10:19, Jesus said, "I have given you authority to trample on serpents and scorpions and over all the power of the enemy, and nothing shall by any means hurt you." (NKJV) Those in Christ are free from the oppression of the enemy!

We know oppression is based in the spirit realm. That is why Jesus used his supernatural power to heal those "oppressed by the devil." Those who are in Christ don't have to suffer spiritual oppression. He died that we might live in freedom. He loves and values us more than we know.

As a child, I didn't see myself as valuable. Therefore, I allowed others to rule over me, eventually allowing Satan to rule over me as well. It wasn't until I allowed God to wrap His loving arms around me that I understood that I am valuable in His sight. When I became a believer, Satan's oppression began to be broken in my life.

II Corinthians 10:4 tells us, "The weapons we fight with are not the weapons of the world. On the contrary, they have divine power to demolish strongholds." (NLT) We truly are in a battle – a battle that takes place in the realm of the spirit. God equips his followers with weapons to defeat the enemy. We have divine power to defeat strongholds.

Spiritually speaking, a stronghold is an area in our lives dominated by Satan. Strongholds will oppress and discourage you, cause you to believe and live in opposition to the kingdom of God, and negatively influence your attitudes and behavior.

125

Amy Mercer

God's truth and God's power are two weapons that must be welcomed into our lives in order to enjoy the freedom from oppression that Christ has called us to live in. His truth will defeat every lie, and His power will defeat every place that the enemy has previously dominated!

Chapter 3

Free From Fear

For God has not given us a spirit of fear, but of power and of love and of a sound mind.

2 TIMOTHY 1:7 NKJV

It was near Halloween, and I was almost five. A group of relatives were gathered around the kitchen table at my aunt's house when the back door opened and in came a figure wearing a white sheet with a white skull-like mask. The mask's teeth were enormous, and the eyes were outlined in black. Sheer terror overtook my senses. I believed some evil creature had invaded our space, and the possibility of death crossed my little mind.

As it turns out, one of my relatives thought it would be funny to play a trick on everyone with the sinister mask and an old bed sheet. Perhaps it was funny to some, but I'll never forget how fear absolutely captivated me in that moment. And while I know that the person dressed up had no intentions of any real harm, I was overtaken with fear. I reasoned that if evil could come that close—even if it was imaginary—it could strike again.

Fear ruled much of my early life. Soon after becoming a believer in Christ, I began understanding that all fear is related to the fear of death. The Lord led me to Hebrews 2:14–15, which says, "Since the children have flesh and blood, He too shared in their humanity so that by His death He might destroy him who holds the power of death—that is, the devil— and free those who all their lives were held in slavery by their fear of death." (NKJV) This makes it clear that Satan has a degree of power—the power of death. His main desire is to kill. However, through Christ we are free from that power. The passage goes on to tell us that many are held in slavery by the fear of death.

If I am afraid of spiders, it is because I ultimately believe that I could be killed by one, or at least severely hurt. The same goes with snakes or any other deadly creature. If someone is afraid of being alone at night, it is rooted in a fear that harm could come that would ultimately end in death.

But as believers, death is not something to be feared. Death is passing into a new and everlasting life, one that will be far greater than life as we know it now. Scripture tells us that death no longer has any sting. We are free from its grips. (1 Corinthians 15:55)

In the meantime, while we reside on Earth, God has given us a wonderful prescription to overcome fear. 2 Timothy 1:7 explains that fear is a spirit. It says, "God has not given us a spirit of fear…" (NKJV) The first bit of good news is that we can identify the source of fear. It is a spirit that comes from the enemy. The second bit of good news comes in the second half of the verse. "...but of power, love, and of a sound mind." (NKJV) God has given us a spirit of power! And he has given us a spirit of love! And he has given us a sound mind! We do not have to be ruled by fear. We can live in peace.

God's love is probably the single most powerful prescription against fear. 1 John 4:18 tells us that "Perfect love casts out fear, because fear has torment." (NKJV) Tormenting fear once ruled me, even in my childhood. But as a follower of Christ, I learned to live free from it. This is knowledge I have to continually apply, because the enemy never stops his assault. He is the ultimate terrorist.

After I gave birth to our two sons, I went through a new challenge with fear. I began to be afraid that something bad would happen to my children. But again, the prescription was the same: allow God's love and power to have a greater place than the feelings of fear.

The opposite of fear is faith. I have had to learn over and over to trust the Lord and to "cast all of my care on Him." (1 Peter 5:7, NKJV) Our faith is built up as we meditate on God's word and as we come to understand His promises.

Fear can take many forms. Anxiety and dread are two forms of fear that must be eradicated from our lives. God wants us to live with the peace of knowing that His plans for us are more powerful than the plans of the enemy, and that if we will submit to God's plan, He will carry us to victory, and we will go in peace.

129

"'For I know the plans I have for you,' declares the LORD, 'plans to prosper you and not to harm you, plans to give you hope and a future.'" (Jeremiah 29:11, NIV)

I am no longer afraid of scary masks, the dark, or the uncertainty of tomorrow. I don't allow my mind to be ruled by the cares of this world. I know the earth as we know it isn't my ultimate home. I am simply passing through, earnestly awaiting the day when Christ will return to Earth. In that day, all fear will be cast away forever!

Chapter 4

Free to Believe

Faith is the confidence that what we hope for will actually happen; it gives us assurance about things we cannot see.

HEBREWS 11:1 NLT

When our second son, Joseph, was ten months old, his pediatrician stretched him out on the examination table and determined that one leg was nearly an inch shorter than the other. We never noticed it since Joseph hadn't started walking yet. But during that rather disappointing doctor's appointment, I saw the stark difference in leg length with my own eyes. The doctor then indicated that the length difference would probably cause Joseph to limp all his life. This was an extra hard blow, since our first son, Luke, had been through several reconstructive surgeries to correct a cleft lip and palate. We had always assumed our second son was perfectly healthy.

The pediatrician set up an appointment for Joseph with an orthopedic specialist. We had about three weeks before meeting with the specialist. In the meantime, I got over the initial devastation and resolved to put Joseph's life in God's hands. I had seen God take care of our every need over and over. So I began to trust Him with this

131

situation as well, and I had an amazing amount of peace. However, I didn't immediately have the faith to believe that God would heal him.

This changed one Sunday morning before church. Those assembled were spending time in prayer, and the man leading spoke these words: "God, it would be nothing for you to make a leg grow longer."

That instant, my faith was renewed, and I believed it, too. Joseph would be healed. I knew it. I had seen God do miraculous things and I had experienced the power of God that often brings instantaneous healing. And I knew that the same God who made Joseph's legs could make one grow to the correct length. But it isn't enough to know that God *can*. Faith is knowing that God *will*. And I knew it.

By the time we took Joseph to the specialist a couple weeks later, his legs were exactly the same length! At his appointment, they x-rayed Joseph's hips to make sure he didn't have a disorder that would have caused his leg to move in and out of socket. But the doctor said that his hips were perfect as well! Today, Joseph's legs are completely even, and he is an active young man with no trouble walking or running.

Both of our sons are healthy, although our oldest has faced many medical challenges. Before Luke was born, my doctor determined that he would be born with a cleft lip. My husband and I went to the ultrasound appointment assuming that the only news we would be getting was whether we were having a healthy boy or girl.

We were shocked by the news of an impending birth defect. We tried to muster our faith, and we prayed for him to be healed in the womb, but with all of our prayer efforts, he was still born with a cleft in both his lip and palate. This is not to say that we've not seen God's hand of healing on Luke's life. He has come a long way, partially through the care and technology of modern medicine, and partially through divine intervention. Many of the issues that accompany clefts could have been much worse, but God has sustained Luke.

I don't understand why I have seen God heal instantaneously at certain times and gradually at other times. But I do know that He is the great Healer who has given us promises we can stand on as His covenant followers.

In the eighth chapter of Luke, a man came to Jesus requesting a miracle for his twelve-year-old daughter who was dying. Jesus began to make his way to her but was thronged by a crowd. He was then touched by a woman with great faith, and she received a miracle of healing. In the meantime, a messenger came from the house where the twelve-year-old girl was dying, and the messenger told the girl's father, "Your daughter is dead. Do not trouble the Teacher." But all hope was not lost. Jesus responded to this seemingly hopeless situation by saying, "Do not be afraid. Only **believe** and she will be made well." Jesus then went to the little girl, took her by the hand, and said, "Little girl, arise." (NKJV)

Jesus made the necessity of belief evident with this very act. In fact, he only allowed those with faith to go into the place where the girl was. The passage also says that Jesus was ridiculed for declaring she was only sleeping, since all medical evidence indicated she was dead. But medical analysis is often trumped by the miracle-working power of God, if we will only believe!

Jesus commands us to believe. We see it over and over in the gospels. In Matthew 21:22, Jesus said, "If you **believe**, you will receive whatever you ask in prayer." (NIV) In Mark 9:23, Jesus said, "Everything is possible for him who **believes**." (NIV) And these are just a couple examples of Jesus emphasizing his desire for us to have faith.

When challenging situations come into my life, I try to immediately put my full trust in God concerning the situation. But I don't ever want to stop there. I want to move beyond trusting Him to believing all of His promises. I want to take an active stance by getting into His word and finding out what He has to say about my situation. I want to actively **believe**!

Chapter 5

Free to Love

**For we know how dearly God loves us, because he has given us
the Holy Spirit to fill our hearts with his love.**
ROMANS 5:5 NLT

Shortly after becoming a believer in Christ, I joined a small
rural church, where I was blessed to be led by pastors and leaders who
had a true heart for God and people. It was a great environment in
which to flourish spiritually. But my ability to form healthy and
meaningful relationships was something I would have to work at for a
long time.

Because of the grace of God, I was able to work through many
areas of hurt and resentment. I was so determined to keep a pure heart
that I took drastic measures when I discovered that I was harboring
feelings of jealousy toward another member of our congregation.

I had a great desire to obey God at all costs, and I knew that
jealousy was an attitude that ran contrary God's standard for believers
who walk in the Spirit (Galatians 5:19–20). So when I began to
harbor this negative attitude, I vowed to fast for three days. I wanted
to be right with God, to be free from the sin that had once entangled
me.

At the start of that three-day period, I got in my car alone and drove two hundred miles down country roads I had never seen before through the southwest portion of Kentucky. At one point, I stopped next to a large lake and talked to the Lord. While perched on large stones that surrounded the water's edge, I sought God with great resolve. I needed to catch a breakthrough from Him. I was determined to have love in my heart toward this particular person at my church – and I was intent on not having jealousy.

Perhaps these were extreme measures to take against just one negative thought pattern. But my mind was set. I was determined to live a holy life. And yes, I could have searched my heart in the privacy of my own apartment, and God would have been faithful to help me. After all, He paid the price so that we might live free from sin. He will help us to walk in the Spirit as we seek Him. However, He also said for us to "work hard to show the results of your salvation, obeying God with deep reverence and fear." (Philippians 2:12, NLT) And the bottom line was this: God had shown me great love, and I was determined to walk in that same love toward Him and others.

I would like to say that I've continuously and consistently sought to deter negative thoughts or attitudes during all of the years since, but the reality is that more times than I care to admit, I have allowed my thoughts, attitudes, and even my actions, to be tainted by fear, bitterness, ingratitude, and selfishness. Life can throw some curve balls. Life can bring unexpected challenges and betrayals. Life can be cruel, and so can people.

But the cruelest event in history is the very event that allows me to love in spite of circumstances. The cruelest event in history was also the most loving. Jesus was mocked, beaten, cursed, and crucified. Yet His response was love.

His love is the only force that allows us to love. His love is here to heal us. His love is here to sustain us. His love is what causes us to flourish and find our real purpose. His love is the very force that has the power to make us brand new.

History has created a great irony. This author, the one penning these very words, the one who literally lost her mind, has been given back her sanity—another chance at life. I am no longer out of my mind. In fact, according to scripture, I have the mind of Christ. (1 Corinthians 2:16) I can think like He thinks. I am no longer living in a mental prison. I am free.

It's not about religion. It *is* about love. And that is the story of my life.

Amy Mercer